Dear Dr G

Keep living the dream!

Thanks for everything.

The
Reservation

Splendid
media group

The Reservation

Martin Montague

Splendid
media group

Published in 2017 by Splendid Media Group (UK) Limited

Splendid Media Group UK Limited
Diamond Suite
The Jubilee Hall
Little Shore Lane
Bishops Waltham
Hampshire SO32 1ED

www.splendidmedia.co.uk

British Library Cataloguing in Publication Data is available from The British Library

978-1-909109-37-7

Editor: Nuala Giblin
Commissioning Editor: Steve Clark
Special thanks to Emma Judd

Designed by Swerve Creative
www.swerve-creative.co.uk

Printed in the UK

Author's note: Some names have been changed in this book

Contents

Prologue

I grew up on a 1970s built council estate in Purbrook, Hampshire. Us locals always referred to it as 'The Reservation' even though there were no big game or Red Indians running around. It was known as the Reservation because of the wide range of people who lived there. Come to think of it, a few of them that I grew up with were like real animals. This is a factual account of growing up and coming of age in the early 90s on the Reservation. It's also a fascinating look at the everyday life and the challenges often faced by those that lived on it.

My journey represents just one of the millions of normally unwritten stories of human misery, dignity, escape and achievement in often remarkable and unseen circumstances of the country's underclasses. I'm certainly no literary genius, but then again this is no novel, so the words here are hardworking, functional and honest ones from my own mouth. My reasons for writing this book are not social or political, it's simply to document and share the often unbelievable stories of life on the Reservation. These events, experiences and places were destined to drift effortlessly into nothing but uncharted, distant memories for those that shared them as we grew up. I strongly believe that sometimes you need to lose yourself to find yourself in life and I certainly did both as I grew up here.

Prologue

The Reservation was like many other council estates that were built in the 1970s. You had row after row and terrace after terrace of houses. They all had white, wooden-clad fronts, dull, grey tiled roofs, metal windows and gardens without fences, spanning several miles. Each house was built identically but was very different in the way they were kept and the people who actually lived there. There were several local parks, some woodland and a few basic shops to cater for the many thousands of local inhabitants.

I imagine some house designer somewhere thought it probably constituted a great design concept to situate so many new families all together with their open plan gardens and allotted green spaces. I'm sure on paper it looked like a great idea but in practice it was a melting pot for an increasing social population. This population explosion had created the need for families to be housed there in the first place. Most families had moved in with small children and now this generation was growing up in numbers that would never be repeated again.

Before I ended up there I lived in Leigh Park, the largest council estate in Europe at the time. We managed to get a council exchange to the Reservation in the spring of 1983 when I was just 10-years-old. I used to be a very scruffy child, with long golden, blonde hair, a fantastic smile and bright blue eyes. I was the youngest of three brothers. My Mum was a single parent who did her best by us and raised the three of us on benefits. So that's the background to my story. And how I ended up on the Reservation.

Chapter One
Burning Summers

It was one of those clear and bright summer mornings in July 1985, as I scrambled out for school and firmly slammed the door shut behind me. I remember looking at the birds in the trees and wishing that I was a bird and could just fly to school. I started to run towards the woods knowing that I would be in a lot of trouble for being late yet again. I am one of those people who really hates being late but I had to carefully time my dash to school to avoid the groups of local bullies who used to chase me. Whenever the bullies would see me, it was like a lion chasing a gazelle across the open plains in Africa. I really felt like I was at the bottom of the food chain and had nothing but my primeval animal instincts and my legs to protect me. To this day I get easily stressed out and I'm sure it's because I had to hone my basic 'fight or flight' instinct at such an early age. If you have ever been bullied in a way that you genuinely feared for your own life, then you will know just how difficult daily survival can be. You will do almost anything to stay well clear of your tormentors.

As I was running towards the woods that separated my house from school, the thought crossed my mind that perhaps I should play truant again. I could hear my battered rucksack straps rattling reassuringly behind me, in a strong rhythmic manner. Hearing that sound meant I was running almost flat out. I hated school and knew that none of my homework was done, yet again. I was a very poor student and never came close to realising my true potential. I would probably get a detention unless I could do it in earlier lessons.

As I got half way through the woods there was a small clearing with an old park in it. Just as I was about to run into the clearing I heard voices: "Look, there's mophead - get him."

Immediately I knew I was in big trouble. My adrenaline started pumping but everything felt like it had gone into slow motion. I was gripped by fear as I literally ran for my worthless little life. I knew the chase was on and I would need to divert every bit of energy I had, as well as completely focus, if I was to have any chance of escape.

In my bid for freedom I ran as fast as I could across the clearing and headed for a fenced alleyway that led to the other side of the park and freedom. I took about another five steps before I was deliberately tripped and fell to the floor. As soon as I hit the ground the gravity of the situation gripped me. Instinctively I knew something bad was about to happen and my heart sank. I rolled into the foetal position as the first kicks from a few Doc Marten boots struck me all over. I yelped, screamed with pain and begged for my life like some kind of coward. But it just made them laugh. They kept kicking with increasing ferocity; the beating felt like it was lasting a lifetime. I closed my eyes and started crying and rolling around in the dirt as I tried to protect my face with my hands.

Burning Summers

One of the boys was Chapman, or Chaps as we called him. Unfortunately I knew him only too well and he held me down with one of his boots. As he stood over me he laughed as he spat on me while the others went through my shabby ex-army rucksack, looking for anything of value. Apart from my schoolbooks I had nothing else worth anything. I got free school dinners because of our circumstances at home and I didn't even have that many pens or pencils. So they just started ripping all my schoolbooks to pieces while I got the odd kick.

Suddenly a voice rang out from someone walking their dog, who could see what was happening, and the bullies fled laughing, leaving me crying on the floor. The dog walker helped me to my feet and asked if I was okay. He then helped me pick up the torn remains of my school books and put them in my bag. "Bloody thugs," he said. I thanked him and he walked off.

I decided I would slowly amble along the last mile or so to school. Whatever the consequences, I had nothing else left to lose. At least I could try to pull myself together. I had cut knuckles from where I had my hands over my face, while being kicked, and I was covered in dirt and spit. I had a big, new hole in the knee of my already shabby and much too small school trousers that some of the other kids at school called ankle swingers.

As I arrived late again my form tutor, Mrs Davies, looked at me almost in disbelief or perhaps sorrow as I was in such a sorry state. She did not even tell me off as she could see I was upset. After the bell rang and everyone left for their first class, she told me to wait behind. Then she asked if everything was alright at home. I said, "Of course Miss, great." She asked what had happened to me. I paused for a split second and thought about telling her. But I imagined the next beating and that would be even more vicious. I replied, "Nothing miss, I just got up late." She gave me a sympathetic yet disbelieving look and just said, in a soft northern voice, "Go and clean yourself up a bit before the next class Martin."

I hated school. All too often I was singled out for being scruffy, dirty, smelly, having long hair or wearing ankle swingers. Poverty is a label that is very difficult to shake off when you are too poor to have regular hot water for baths, clean clothes or even money for a haircut. Often I used to look out the window at school and daydream about being a millionaire; having a big house and a sports car and showing everyone that I was perfectly capable of making my own luck. One day I would escape this place. Daydreaming was about the only thing I was good at. I mentally escaped school each and every day as often as I could. I remember another one of my teachers, also called Davies but he was a mister, who taught computer studies, saying that the only thing I would ever be good for, when I was older, was a 'biro mechanic'. It was due to the fact that I used to nervously sit there playing with my pens in my teeth.

Fortunately, the summer holidays were only days away and I was already anticipating the adventures I would have. But I also felt a deep loathing for losing all my friends from Leigh Park, barely a year or so before, and being bullied on a regular basis. I had several really good friends; one was called Paul Ashcroft and another was Paul Richardson. We used to spend hours playing in the local woods and I never got bullied there. I was even top of my class at infants' school and used to really enjoy it. But now, since the move, I was being forced to live like a coward, to avoid the pain and unwanted attention my social situation used to bring.

Although hardly religious my Mum had had me 'crash' christened so I could go to a Roman Catholic school called Oaklands RC Comprehensive in Purbrook. It was a nice school as schools go. Originally an all-girls school run by nuns, it had ended up being a mixed comprehensive. The school was based around an old cream coloured house with an assortment of other buildings that had been added over the years. It was fairly strict compared to other schools at the time. The problem was that although it provided me with better education opportunities - as schools near the Reservation go - very few of the kids from the Reservation actually went there. It was a religious school so I was singled out as a Bible Basher. This only added to the long list of reasons to single me out for a beating.

My social circle of new friends was a spatter of people from school who lived on or near the Reservation. Along with others who lived near me who I'd become friendly with over the previous year at my last year in middle school.

On the way home I thought, "I'm not going back this term." I hoped the bullying might go away during the long summer holidays. So I bunked off the remaining few days and spent the vast majority of the time in our shed at home, or hiding in the woods. Doing this was risky as the educational welfare officer had already been round my house asking about my truancy. And when I was in the woods I still had to avoid any of the bullies who were also bunking off. I would have to go all day without any food because I used to get free school meals. But it was worth it, as I counted down the last few days to the start of the summer holidays.

This, like every other summer holiday, was spent 'trundling' or cycling around the Reservation on our BMX bikes, trying to entertain ourselves. This would often consist of going camping on Purbrook Heath or in one of a few abandoned houses we knew of. I had about five people that I would call close childhood friends. Typically, at least one of us had run away from home at any particular time over the holidays. Escaping from one family problem or another.

One of these friends was Phil but we called him Cotton. He was an accomplished shop lifter and used to drop in at a shop called W.E King's in Widley to steal a range of chocolate, alcohol and porn magazines to help pass the time around the camp fire. Cotton was street savvy from an early age and very rugged. He had fair, bushy curly hair and would always get stuck into a fight if he ever got picked on. Cotton had a really tough time at home. His Dad was from Ireland and was not only a serious disciplinarian but also a raging alcoholic. Cotton never had his own bedroom so he used to sleep on the sofa or floor at home like some kind of dog. His Dad would come home from the pub and literally beat him black and blue just for the twisted fun of it.

Cotton often turned up at my house without a shirt or shoes on, usually after he had done something wrong and had to run away from home. Out of my close friends I really think Cotton had the worst of it. He was both mentally abused and physically beaten by his Dad on an all too regular basis. Things could get very tough for me with bullying but I never had to deal with any kind of abuse at home.

Burning Summers

Whenever the police went round, we all thought his Dad would go too far and one day literally beat him to death. His Dad used to make him recite the Bible while he battered him with his belt to the point he would almost pass out. Over and over again he would strike him with his leather belt with the metal buckle on the end. It must have been agonising. His Dad often found it satisfying to make him kneel down and pray for forgiveness with his hands together while he repeatedly struck him with the belt or punched him.

Often, when getting changed for PE, you couldn't help noticing that Cotton was covered in a range of yellow or fresher, black, bruising. I remember looking at him one day and thinking I'm not sure how I would cope with that. Nevertheless he was almost always cheerful and managed to more or less look after himself by stealing clothes from local washing lines or trainers from Hilsea Lido when people went for a swim. I remember on one occasion walking through Waterlooville town centre with Cotton when someone came up and demanded he give his top back. He had only stolen it off of this lad's washing line. Cotton was ashamed so handed it over and wanted to avoid any unnecessary beating from this older lad. He then had to walk home in the dead of winter and in the rain without a top on.

Another day he had got a pen knife from somewhere. He ran up to a tree and went to stab it into the bark, but instead of the knife going in the tree, it slipped and stabbed him in the leg. With most of the blade embedded in his leg. He stood there, realising he would have to pull it out. I watched as he did and a torrent of bright red blood started running down his leg.

The Reservation

It was a really deep stab wound but all we could do was compress it to try and stop the bleeding. It really needed stitches but no one had any way of getting to the hospital as none of us had a car. And Cotton was worried about getting into trouble so an ambulance was out of the question. Fortunately, after quite a long time the bleeding slowed down and as he had missed all the arteries, so he never bled out. But this simple accident could have ended up being fatal.

In a last minute change from camping on the Heath, we all decided to camp in a deserted house behind a very high wall that stood on the side of Stakes Road, right behind a petrol station and next to a church. I believe the half derelict place we were in used to be something to do with a large old Vicarage that was still in use and close to the church. It was an old Victorian or Edwardian building that we were all hiding in. It was a rather elegantly designed period house with large windows and spacious rooms.

It was not really derelict but not used either; it was somewhere in-between. The doors were always open so gaining entry was not a problem once you had scaled the wall adjoining the petrol station. I was with Cotton, Fizz, Dale, Swain and Gal. Everyone had nicknames. The one thing that kids knew how to do was to give each other the most hideous nicknames. I was known as Monty or Mophead because my hair was always long and a dishevelled mess. But I remember some of the local kids having nicknames like, 'Big eared boss eyed bastard' or 'The Trog' and so on.

The house was completely empty except for piles of old school-style chairs. I imagine they were only used for summer fetes that were held in the formal grounds of the Vicarage. The house seemed like a great place to camp for the night. We decided the warmest and safest place to sleep would be up in the loft. That way we wouldn't be visible through the bare windows to the building opposite. Otherwise we could probably be seen in the downstairs rooms from about 200 yards away. We all put our sleeping bags up there and set up a paraffin lamp. Then we started drinking a bottle of very bitter and still fermenting home brew that I had taken from home. We affectionately called it Gut Wrench.

For breakfast we used to leave notes for the Milkman, in the early hours of the morning, on nearby doorsteps; we always did this whenever we were camping out anywhere. For example, 'Please can you leave bacon today' or 'Can I have some eggs or bread today?' I had gone out with Dale to place some of these notes in preparation for feeding us after the early morning milk round. Dale was very tall for his age and towered over the rest of us. He had dark, flicked hair and was always well-dressed. Dale considered himself a bit of a ladies' man and was really into football. He lived off the Reservation and his Dad had been in the Navy.

Dale was rich by our standards because his parents owned their own house, which even had a garage and a fitted kitchen. Dale was always very amiable and willing; later in life this eagerness to please and amiable nature would be his downfall. He was always up for a bit of a 'trundle' to put the Milkman notes out. That morning we left to go and place the notes as usual. It was just before dawn as we slipped the notes into empty milk bottles on people's doorsteps. As we headed back to the house we both stopped to appreciate the warm morning glow and the light in front of us. Then we realised it couldn't be sunrise at this time of the morning, even in mid-summer. We both looked at each other. The speechless expression on our faces and hollow eyes said it all. After a pause, which felt like forever, Dale finally spoke: "Fuck, the wankers have burnt the house down."

The gravity of the situation immediately dawned on me as I started shaking like a leaf in the wind and my legs turned to jelly. As we ran closer thoughts of Fizz and Cotton being burnt alive crossed my mind. I ran to a local phone box and dialled 999. I was hyperventilating and could barely get any words out as I said, "Fire, right behind the petrol station in a house on London Road, Purbrook." I immediately hung up. Dale and I noticed three dishevelled figures running towards us in the darkness as the police and fire brigade turned up. It was Gal, Fizz and Cotton. It was like a eureka moment as we jumped for joy, knowing they were all still alive. We then ran swiftly away from the scene. We could see how serious the situation was as the burning house was literally right next to the petrol station. You did not need to be a rocket scientist to realise that if the petrol station went up there would be a massive explosion and potential loss of life.

We stopped far enough away that we could see the vague outlines of what was happening but hopefully would not be associated with the fire. Everyone was arguing over exactly what had happened and everyone was denying it was them. They knew just how serious it was. However, it was clear that a solid fuel camping stove, that was being used to cook food up in the loft, had set fire to the loft insulation and the whole place had gone up in flames. Everyone agreed we should never talk about it to anyone and just deny it emphatically if we were ever asked.

Over the coming days the fire at the old house was the talk of the Reservation. Rumours circulated about it being a tramp or arson. Someone mentioned to me that it had been in the local paper and that whoever did this would be locked up for a very long time. I just laughed, walked away and was sick. I feared being put into a Home even though I wasn't there when the place actually caught fire but I was clearly associated with it. There was no way on earth I ever wanted to be another Oliver Twist.

After a week or two we had almost forgotten about it. Unless, of course, we walked past and were reminded by the charred remains of roof joists and stained black rubble, which was visible if you looked over the wall. The rest of the summer holidays passed reasonably uneventfully. We would hang out sitting on the beams of a local church's outside porch. getting drunk or playing the game Murder in the Dark in the graveyard at night. It was basically like Hide and Seek but as soon as you were found you got jumped by everyone else. We used to sit there drinking Gut Wrench or anything else we could get our hands on. To this day I can't bear the smell of gin as Cotton stole a bottle from somewhere he burgled and we were all so sick on it that I have a lifelong hate of the stuff.

At the very end of the holidays Dale and I stayed around Fizz's house. He lived fairly close to me on the Reservation near a large smelly pond. It was basically a hole in the ground, about 200 feet wide and had probably been a feature when the estate was built. But now it was just full of algae, frames from stolen bikes and Tesco trolleys. Fizz was always saying how he was going to go out with some really pretty girl or other but never did. He had wavy, blonde hair and was very opinionated and outspoken. I always thought he should be a politician or something like that when he grew up because he loved to debate everything in detail. His Mum was originally from the Seychelles and he had two sisters. Tina, the older one had long, dark curly hair and a figure to die for. We all used to enjoy going to his house to catch a glimpse of her. She was certainly one of the best looking attractions on the Reservation. Tina used to be a hostess on the Isle of Wight ferry at Southsea.

One night we all got super drunk on Kestrel Super Strength. Dale had a fairly plentiful supply of money as his parents weren't too badly off and Fizz was quite persuasive so was able to tap into this source. Dale could conjure up some strange reasons why people should give him some money. Failing that, his Dad used to collect customers' money for the Co-op and he used to just help himself.

Getting served was always a problem because we were only the tender age of twelve or thirteen. But we had devised a solution for it. I would borrow my older brother's spare crash helmet with a tinted visor, then simply run in the shop wearing it on my head and holding some keys in my hand. I'd go over to the Kestrel Super Strength, pick it up, put it on the counter and pay for it using a deep voice. I was never ever asked for ID so we always got served. We'd always drink far more than we could handle. Kestrel Super Strength was like drinking high alcohol tar; the stuff was absolutely lethal.

Before we went to Fizz's that night, my Mum had cooked us

one of her special homemade curries. I say 'special', but not in a good way. Mum's curries were basically leftovers with curry powder and rice, all mixed together, but the boys seemed to enjoy it. To give you an example of my Mum's culinary skills, she once got a job at an old people's home but lasted just one day before the residents bitterly complained and got her fired.

Before hitting the Kestrel Super Strength at Fizz's we had already been on the Gut Wrench at mine so it was a lethal combination. I was chatting to Dale in Fizz's room when all of a sudden he started acting funny but we just laughed at him. He roamed around stumbling and mumbling to himself before he returned with a large carving knife and started waving it around, demanding we be quiet. Dale just kept laughing at him but then Fizz tried to stab him with the knife in his drunken rage. We managed to disarm him but then he walked off again and came back a few moments later with a toilet brush. He said: 'If either of you makes any more noise I am going to shove this right up your arse."

We all had a laugh and then went to sleep. In my drunken stupor I could hear Fizz being sick pretty much all night.

First thing in the morning we were awoken to the sound of his Mum screaming and banging on his door at the top of her voice. She was screaming: "You little shit, fucking clean all that bloody sick up, you are no son of mine." The bathroom was completely full of Gut Wrench with curry. It was foul and that red Gut Wrench sure did stain. But the worst thing was that in the end he'd obviously decided to be sick out of his bedroom window, instead of bothering to go to the bathroom. So now the white-clad front of the council house was covered in bright red streaks of Gut Wrench with bits of rice stuck to it.

His Mum was still screaming as we swiftly left and was hitting him continually. As Dale and I headed for home I reminded him, "School tomorrow. That summer went quickly." He just said: "I have some porn mags at mine if you wanna come and look? I stole them from my Dad."

We just laughed and went our separate ways, both dreading going back to school the next day.

Chapter Two
The Lines

Swain lived off the Reservation in Cosham. He was heavy set with very thick, dark hair and when he got excited he would put his hands in his pockets and shake them around. It almost looked like he was masturbating and it was a habit he never grew out of, as long as I knew him. We got more and more friendly at school and used to jump over the fence at break times and go for a cigarette in the thick woodland that adjoined the school. The hidden smoking spot was by the Maths and Science block and used to get busier every year as more of the kids came for a smoke. Often at lunch time we used to roam around the woods. Deep inside there was a large lake called Diggers Pond. It was called this because it had recently been excavated by large diggers to make it into some kind of feature.

One day at lunchtime we all thought it would be hilarious to get a load of old clothes and stuff them full of twigs and long grass and make a mannequin. We even tied gloves to it, put some old trainers on and a mask; it looked almost human! Previously we had found an inflatable canoe nearby, which was poorly hidden, so we took it and hid it somewhere else. Now we dragged both the canoe and the mannequin to the side of the lake and set about inflating the canoe. We took turns blowing it up while we shared cigarettes. When it was inflated enough to float, two of us went out on the water, along with the mannequin.

When we got to the centre of the lake, I tied some rope to the belt loop on the front of the mannequin's jeans and tied the other end of the rope to one of those household bricks that had holes running through them. I then threw the mannequin and the brick overboard. It really looked like the drowned body of a child was floating in the water. At this point we had set the trap for the afternoon's amusement as we bunked off double PE.

After we dragged the canoe away we sat hidden in the undergrowth waiting for any passers-by who were using the footpath. The first came along with his dog and immediately ran to the side of the lake and shouted: "Are you ok?"

You could tell he wasn't quite sure if it was a dead body and now he was getting more and more agitated. He took his shoes off and rolled up his trousers to see how deep it was. This lake was extremely muddy. It was the kind of mud you sunk straight into and it was several metres deep in the middle. The passer-by walked into the water until he started to sink. So he retreated to the bank and sat for a minute pondering what to do. After a few minutes he stood up and had another look at the floating body, jumped up to try to get a better look and then put his shoes and socks back on and rapidly left.

We all thought this was absolutely hilarious as we sat hidden, smoking and laughing to ourselves. About five or ten minutes later a woman with a pram came from the other direction. She also stopped to look at our drowned body but then slowly continued onwards. Then a few kids who were also bunking off from school came along. They had quite the opposite reaction. Rather than seeing if they could help, they thought they'd check to see if it was real by throwing stones at it.

As they threw their stones, the first guy with his dog came running back down the hill with a policeman; the school kids made a hasty retreat. The policeman started to run frantically around the lake, trying to look at it. He then used his radio to call for assistance, fearing the worst. We crept back a little further into the undergrowth and watched as more police turned up. Lots and lots of them.

At this point we decided we needed to scarper back to the school grounds so we never got caught. In afternoon registration we could hear a raft of sirens and emergency vehicles going past the school and making their way into the woods. Our little practical joke had got way out of proportion. At least it was only a handmade mannequin. But we were all seriously scared we would get found out, as this was rapidly turning into a major rescue operation. But we never did.

A few of us started going down to Cosham after school with Swain and would play on Hilsea Lines. The Lines were some old Victorian fortifications that were meant to protect us from invasions. We used to dream of breaking in and discovering wartime treasures and exploring the underground network of tunnels.

Swain's Dad was a solicitor who spent a lot of time away from home so his house made a great truant spot and backed onto a Masonic Lodge. One day, to our delight, we discovered a large delivery of alcohol which had been left outside the back of the

Lodge. We stole the entire consignment and everyone got really drunk every day for weeks and weeks. We had all kinds of beer, wines and spirits and every day at school we used to say to each other, "Let's get pissed," and laughed, knowing we had a stockpile of hidden alcohol that was enough to run a pub.

I can remember once I was playing truant round Swain's when there was a knock on the door. We all hid as a voice shouted through the letterbox saying, "I know you are in there, this is the education welfare officer". Right there and then everyone thought, oh my God, that's not good. We were all playing truant and had been admiring the mouldy, home brew container that we used to be sick in. We had just put the lid back on and were all fairly drunk from our ill-gotten goods when Swain calmly said, "Go away, I am ill." The voice insisted he open the door but Swain stood his ground and repeated that he was ill. And he was definitely not allowed to talk to any adult strangers. Finally, the officer had no option but to give up and leave.

Now the coast was clear we headed off to explore Hilsea Lines. It was great fun. You could explore numerous bits and there were old gun emplacements and brick-built corridors and courtyards. It was amazing. We found a business nearby that had loads of really cool helicopter parts and military surplus in the yard. It adjoined the Lines at the back and had a high wall covered with glass and vandal-proof paint. We snapped all the glass off with a school jumper and then climbed into the yard to grab some souvenirs. After filling our pockets with all sorts of weird and wonderful stuff we heard a voice ringing out, "Oi you little bastards." In a hell of a rush to escape, the first two climbed up the pallets inside the yard, and jumped off the wall, onto the grass bank on the other side. Swain got on top of the wall and turned to look, just as someone threw a lump of metal at him. He fell 10 foot or so onto the grass bank the other side, clutching his face.

Swain had been hit so hard that his nose was smashed to bits and there was blood pouring out and going all over him. He was drenched in blood. His hands were clutching his face and the blood was dripping down his arms to the end of his elbows. He was in an awful mess and this was the most blood that I had ever seen in my life. We dragged him away because we didn't want to get caught by the police or the angry and clearly violent yard worker. Swain just wanted to stay there but we knew we had to leave as fast as possible to avoid more trouble.

It was definitely a hospital job so we took him to the Queen Alexandra Hospital. We made our excuses to leave as soon as we could to reduce the chances of being asked awkward questions. Swain's clothes must have been ruined and his nose looked a terrible mess for quite some time afterwards. I remember that later he had to have it straightened and he had black eyes for ages. In fact, Swain almost looked like a panda for several weeks.

As I walked home via the long and steep Portsdown Hill, I met up with Neil and Chaps. Chaps was one of the kids who had been bullying me a few years before, but for the last year or so had left me alone in favour of other poor souls. They were just off to the viewpoint at the top of the hill, to look for any old spliff butts that they could re-roll to get stoned on. Neil's house was directly behind mine on the Reservation and Chaps's was a few minutes' walk away from ours. Neil was often referred to as The Incredible

Bullshitting Man by the locals or The Storyteller. He had longish, flicked, dark brown hair and always used to dress in a very late 80s, acid raver, Happy Mondays kind of way. I asked how he was and he replied: "Yeah man, sorted, we did 2, 5, no, 10 trips last night and are just going up the hill. You coming?" At that moment Chaps looked over and said: "For fuck's sake Neil, you are so full of shit. We had half a trip each. 'Ere Monty, have you got any gear?" I said no and he said: "Shame," and started walking off.

The fact is I had never even smoked dope. It was kind of a new thing that people were just starting to discover on the Reservation. However, most people on the Reservation would do anything they could to escape for a while, either physically or mentally. Pretty much everyone I know used to sniff petrol at the time, me included. I'm certainly not proud of it but it happened, and this is a warts and all account of my experiences growing up. So despite my own personal feelings on the matter, I have included it here.

I never sniffed glue or gas. It was common knowledge that people had died doing it. But looking back I'm sure petrol sniffing was probably far worse for you and a much more localised problem than a national one. Basically you would siphon some into a can, pour a bit on a rag and then inhale through it for a bit. Before you knew it you had a really thick buzz with a tune playing in your head. I think the tune was probably the billions of brain cells being systematically destroyed and screaming for you to stop. It would then lead to a massive trip and you would see all sorts of crazy things happening, rooms breathing and so on. Very, very nasty stuff and in hindsight, the worst thing I have ever done to get high. When you inhale petrol you have no idea what kind of buzz it can give you. And there is virtually no way to police the potential abuse because the stuff is so readily available.

Petrol sniffing on the Reservation was all too frequent. Children from about nine or ten years of age could often be seen sniffing petrol in the woods and smoking. I remember regularly seeing people so off their heads from sniffing petrol, that they would nearly kill themselves while riding around the estate on stolen motorcycles. And there was often a strong smell of petrol on everyone's clothes.

My Mum used to have an old Honda Express moped and one day I walked out the house to see one of the local scumbag kids out cold, draped over it. His mouth was still French kissing the petrol tank. I shook him a few times and moved him until he started to regain consciousness. Part of me wished he was dead because he was such a bully and trouble maker, even by Reservation standards. As he came round he just grinned and ran off like a drunken man, zig-zagging towards his house. That was the scale of the abuse. Anything petrol-wise, that could be sniffed, was sniffed. Cars' petrol tanks were siphoned off and almost every kid I knew was doing it. There was a period of time when almost everything motorised would struggle to get off the Reservation because it was being drained bone dry.

One day I witnessed a group of kids pushing a long rag into a petrol tank with a twig. While they prized the filler cap off, a couple stood there smoking. To this day I am amazed no one, to my knowledge, got blown to bits or seriously burnt.

One evening Neil and Chaps knocked on my door and I thought, just go away. Neil was okay and friendly enough but

The Reservation

Chaps was a real troublemaker. I had the misfortune of spending a year at middle school sitting next to him, before he turned bully on me. He often used to draw people bleeding or paint only all-black pictures. He was very shifty and really lacked any boundaries. He would often marvel over dead animals in the woods and be extremely spiteful towards people's cats. He was just the kind of kid who would walk up to someone and hit them for a laugh. I guess he had some faulty wiring or something or just soaked up a little too much of the Reservation.

After I didn't open the door the pair opened the side gate and let themselves into the back garden. I stayed completely still, pretending not to be in, when I heard Chaps say to Neil, "He's fucking out, let's smash the window with a brick and rob the place." As he bent down to pick up, an old brick I knew what was coming so I opened the door and said, "Sorry guys I was in the bath. Great to see you both." Chaps went straight to the kitchen and turned the gas cooker on and then helped himself to two knives out of the drawer. Then he took a clean milk bottle from beside the sink, put a coin in it and shook the bottle until the bottom smashed. Finally, he heated some knives and when they were red hot put some dope on them. He pressed them together and inhaled the smoke through the top of the broken bottle. This, I later found out, was called 'Hot Knives'.

Half an hour later they were both sat slumped in my lounge, watching the film Weird Science on TV. My Mum later asked why all the knives in the kitchen drawer had burnt ends. I kept trying to get rid of the two of them but it was futile and they knew it all too well. Chaps kept saying, "I am on cloud nine man, Neil skin up." Neil then rolled a joint from the spliff butts that they'd found earlier on top of the hill and after they'd smoked most of it, they offered me some. I was initially reticent, as I was not one to just go along with people, but after some coercion I decided to try it. Nothing seemed to happen. I remember I was watching Weird Science and there is a scene where someone is turned into a creature with a long tongue. All of a sudden I found myself laughing uncontrollably and felt so calm and relaxed. From that point on we all seemed to be sharing a bubble and I kind of connected with them. Even Chaps seemed temporarily human.

That was my first experience of smoking pot and over the following months it became far too common amongst us kids on the Reservation. But it was a most welcome replacement to all the petrol sniffing that had been going on previously. And at least a few more motorists could get to work without running out of fuel as suddenly, there was a plentiful supply on the Reservation.

That year was memorable for another reason. It was the evening of the 15th of October 1987 and I had gone to bed as usual when I was awoken by the wind rattling around the house. I had never heard gusts of wind like it. Despite all the windows being closed the drafts of compressed air, pushing through the gaps, were making a high pitched squeal and hurt your ears as they built up during the evening. No one had mentioned on TV that this storm was going to be so severe so I just assumed it was a normal storm. It was so noisy I couldn't sleep and I could hear the cat out in the front garden meowing to be let in. I got up and opened the door but the second I undid the catch, to let the cat in, the door was ripped from my fingertips. The door came towards me with such ferocity that it knocked me backwards into the hallway. And the wind that whistled by my ears made it feel like I was in some kind of wind tunnel.

I got to my feet and despite the force of the wind, between gusts, I managed to get into the front garden. The scene was surreal and unlike anything I had ever seen before. The cat tried to run towards me but was lifted clear off the ground in a gust of wind and taken sideways across the garden and then dropped down. I tried to make it towards the poor cat but it really was like being in a wind tunnel. Every time you got hit with a gust you were either knocked to the floor or blown sideways and I had to cling to one of the bushes in the front garden.

Mum was screaming for me to come in but I was determined to get the cat. After several more anti-gravity attempts by both of us, I managed to grab the cat and bring it safely into the house. From indoors you could hear the loud shrieking and cracking of the trees nearby as they either had their branches ripped off or they were uprooted completely.

The wind continued to rattle and squeal around the whole house as it tried to force its way in. Some of the gusts that night got up to around 120 mph and it was a one in every two-hundred-year freak storm. As things slowly started to ease up I managed to get a little sleep. In the morning I got up for school as usual and Dale and Cotton knocked for me on the way. They eagerly said, "You got to see it out here." There were houses with roofs ripped off and one of the huts was turned over at the middle school near Cotton's.

By the time we got to the local woods it was apparent that

this was not a normal storm. As we drew closer you could see upturned trees with large root packs ripped out of the ground and facing skywards. There were tree limbs strewn across all the paths on the way to school. As we passed the woods and walked through the new estate nearby, you could see tree limbs poking out of people's lofts, large branches in their gardens and several cars covered in trees or large branches. This new estate had taken quite a beating. It was right in the middle of this woodland so was surrounded by old oak trees on all sides.

It was a very exciting walk to school that day and when we got there it was apparent that the school had also sustained some serious damage. One of the main blocks and a few huts had been damaged. It was eerily quiet and a teacher came up to us and told us that school was closed for the day. We couldn't be happier as we made our way back home again.

On the way back, through that new estate that had been hit so hard, we helped someone move a large branch that was blocking their drive. And then to our surprise they gave us some money to drag it along the alleyway and dump it in the woods. Then no sooner had the three of us done this when somebody else asked for help, then another and another. We spent the best part of the day in that road getting paid to shift tree limbs, branches and rubbish. I felt particularly sorry for one of the home owners who had a whole tree resting on her house after it had fallen and smashed its way through the roof. By the time we got home we had split the money and had enough for some alcohol and food. So we decided we should go camping that night.

The Reservation

We had a couple of spots we used to enjoy going to. We particularly liked a few spots on Purbrook Heath. It was fairly near a river and under a large tree that had a 'U' shaped bend in it. The other one was a little further on between a lot of scrub but it was a bit soggy so we decided to camp at our normal spot. We lugged the alcohol, along with the sleeping bags and a few tins of food to the site and set up camp. We never used tents. More often than not we would just stay up chatting all night and then go home to bed.

After the sun's red glow went down behind the trees we set about telling ghost stories around the fire and sipping beer. Cooking was always the highlight of the evening. We would have tins of beans and sausages or spaghetti hoops and stuff like that. Breakfast was always made up of whatever we could get the Milkman to deliver in the morning like bacon, bread and eggs. It had been somewhat of an on-going joke that if anyone fell asleep, we would throw an unopened tin of food onto the fire. Once the tins were hot enough they would explode with a massive bang. So you would have a combination of flying red hot metal, food and fire embers going in several directions. I'm sure you must have been able to hear these explosions a mile or two away as they were so loud.

Tonight it was Dale who had fallen asleep so I threw a tin of Fizz spaghetti hoops on the fire. He got the right ass as he wanted to eat them. I said don't worry, you can have a tin of luncheon meat. He replied, "Yum," and I threw it to him. He looked at it for a minute by the flickering light of the fire and commented that the label was missing. With a straight face I said it was fine, it must have just come off. And added, "Don't worry, it's lovely.

Seriously, try it." He took the lid off with a can opener, sniffed it, then grabbed a fork and started tucking in.

Initially he was a bit apprehensive but after a few mouthfuls he started saying, "Nice," and you could see him eating it faster and faster like an animal. The fork could be heard enthusiastically rattling on the sides of the can as he devoured it. Then Cotton chirped up and said, "Fizz, that fucker's just given you a can of dog food." I immediately started laughing. I had bought it on the way and taken the label off in the hope that someone would eat it. Cotton had seen me taking the label off a bit earlier, pointed at Fizz and just smiled. The minute he knew it was dog food he started retching and ran about twenty or so yards. You could hear him being sick.

As we were laughing there was an almighty explosion. This massive bang was the tin of spaghetti hoops that I had thrown on the fire when Dale fell asleep about half an hour earlier. All the embers from the fire went flying everywhere and we were all surprised by just how much this tin had blown up. Dale suddenly screamed and leapt to his feet, covering his face. He was screaming in agony after he had been abruptly woken up and hit in the face. We assumed the worst for a split second thinking that a piece of the red hot exploding metal had struck him in the face as he slept.

After Dale had stopped jumping around and removed his hands from his face, we all laughed as he was covered in boiling hot spaghetti hoops. And it was sauce not blood on his face. The hoops were stuck all over his face and were still really hot. Dale kept asking, "Am I cut? Am I ok?" I must admit I breathed a sigh of relief even though he was screaming and going mental and was desperate to find out who was responsible.

As soon as the sun came up we had some bacon and eggs a Milkman had left (not for us!) and then headed off for the long walk back to the Reservation. On the way we walked past a car with some keys in it. It was still so early that there was a morning mist. Cotton had noticed the keys on the passenger seat and tried all the doors but the car was locked. We all told him to leave it alone and continued to walk on but he insisted, "I'm a professional, don't worry. We can learn how to drive on the way and it will save walking."

We were about 100 yards ahead when we heard the sound of smashing glass. Cotton had found a rock and thrown it through the window. It soon became apparent that the keys in the car were not actually for that car. Exactly as we had told him and the whole thing had been a needless act of vandalism. All Cotton got from the car was a couple of Showaddywaddy tapes and a box of matches. But as he ran to catch up he was ripping the tape from the cassettes and then just threw them away.

About five or ten minutes further up the road the police stopped us as there had been a burglary reported locally. I thought we were all going to get collared for the car but it soon became apparent that it was a house burglary. They asked us what we had been doing, where we were going and then got us all to empty out our sleeping bags. You could hear the clatter but it was only knives, forks can openers and stuff. They then took a pocket notebook out and asked us all for our names.

When the copper got to Dale he asked, "What you done to your face?" as some of the spaghetti hoops had burnt him. When he explained we all laughed but the copper never so much as grinned. He then asked Dale his surname and when he told him it was Brown, which was his real name, the copper said, "No, your real name sonny not the 'Brown one." Over the next ten minutes there was a heated discussion about the fact that it really was his name. Finally, we were able to be on our way.

As usual, the moment I got home I fell asleep with my hands and face still black and stinking of smoke from the fire.

The Reservation

Chapter Three
Poverty

Now what can I tell you about poverty? Well poverty is also a question of perspective. There is always someone in a better or worse situation than you. If you take two starving people and give one an apple he will think he is a rich man. I think poverty is a combination of a wide range of factors over a long time. I would class my own experiences of dealing with poverty in a number of different ways. But let me just say that poor people don't often see themselves as being poor, because they associate with lots of people in a similar situation, in similar surroundings.

Anyone on the breadline will tell you that when you are poor the most important thing is food. Hence why it's known as being on the breadline. Most of the time we had enough to eat. Okay, the food could be bad and at times consisted of nothing but jacket potatoes with no topping but it was enough to sustain you. You would be surprised that even a plain potato, five nights on the trot for dinner, felt like a feast when, on the sixth night, you had beans on it.

This was topped up with free school dinners. And when Mum had a little money we would have a small piece of steak once every few weeks, on a Friday night. Don't get me wrong, most of the time we weren't living on jacket potatoes every night. It was usually only when something had gone wrong with the Housing Benefit or something similar. I was lucky enough to eat every single day, more or less the whole of my life. But I think the first thing the more fortunate take for granted has to be food.

Ask anyone who's poor about what their other priorities are and they will always say electric. We spent the whole time on slot meters. Unlike the keys today you couldn't borrow anything. If you ran out of money, you ran out of electric or gas; it was as simple as that. If it meant going a day without then that was the way it had to be. But these utilities were rationed and often stretched to the limit to avoid sitting in total darkness. Things I take for granted today were once things I longed for on a daily basis.

Hot water is one of the rarest and most precious commodities when you are on the breadline. We were not allowed to have the heater on without asking first and often it would be only lukewarm or turned off completely to save electricity. It was a case of a bath once a week. And as we only had it on the lowest setting, the heater would only heat a little water at the top of the tank, so you would only get about 4 inches' worth of hot water in the bath.

Heating was another luxury that I now take for granted. Being brought up in a constantly cold house could prove challenging at times. We had central heating but never ever had it on as it was electric and we couldn't afford it. There was a Calor gas fire in the lounge and we'd have gas bottles delivered so we could have a gas fire on. There were prolonged periods without gas, and again, when the fire was on, it was rationed to one bar. Occasionally we would have three on. I remember huddling around the fire, shivering after a tepid bath and trying to get warm.

Poverty

Winters could be especially cruel when you are too poor to have any heating on or hot water. I remember often having to go to bed in my school clothes to keep warm. And curling up into a tiny ball and putting my head under the covers so my breath would warm me up. It was not uncommon to see ice on both sides of the windows in my bedroom, and wake up in the morning and be able to see your own breath in the stark, frigid air.

Unsurprisingly, as a child, I always suffered far more bad colds or chest infections compared to a lot of other children at school. Looking back, it was hardly a surprise but you got used to it. Sometimes I would boil a kettle to wash my hair, hands or face properly before school. I would say that poverty can come in many shapes or forms, but I would also say these childhood hardships have been character building. And I vividly remember that when we rented our first house with heating and hot water, it felt like we had finally entered Middle England.

Poor people still celebrate Christmas, they still laugh, cry and breathe. Being poor is not a choice for a lot of children, they are simply born into it. The same can be said for those from richer families. We are moulded by our surroundings and our own moral compasses, along with the choices we make and the drive we have to effect change.

I remember someone saying to me that they had a tough time as a child. Their parents would have to get loans to take them on holiday and often they would worry about paying the mortgage and getting what they wanted for Christmas. I just stood there and thought, you really have no idea. You had holidays and your own house? And I bet you had hot water and heating plus a car.

The Reservation

One of those things on wheels that most families near me could only dream about... poor old you. But instead I just said, "That must have been terrible," and changed the subject. This is exactly what I mean about perspective, I know things were tough as a kid, but lots of people had it a lot tougher. Poverty should never be made out to be some middle class crisis about having to take out a loan for a holiday or to buy a home. How do you make people understand the difference?

My Mum would buy one thing a week for Christmas and hide it away. Now, as an adult Christmas means very little to me because if I want something I simply go and buy it. But as a child it was the time of dreams. We'd put the decorations up a week or so before. We'd decorate the tree and invariably try to get the broken lights to work. It was such an exciting time of year. For a few days all your hopes and dreams somehow seemed possible. On Christmas Eve we were allowed to eat the chocolate coins on the trees. And my Mum would put some bowls out in the dining room with nuts in.

Christmas is a great time for bringing families and friends together. Today I really hate the overly political correctness of it all. As a child, things always seem so much simpler. We would watch TV and I would always go to bed far too early to try to speed up the arrival of Christmas Day. I would wake up at about 4am in the morning and spend the whole day marvelling at the goodies I had received. I always really hated going back to school after the holidays. Even at a young age Christmas seemed so materialistic as everyone compared what they had got.

While growing up I only had two dreams. The first was that one day I would meet my Dad. He had left while my Mum was pregnant with me. So when I was in my mid 20s I got a company to trace him and found out he lived fairly close to me, in a nice house about ten miles up the road. When I was given the details by the chap who traced him, he said: "Remember, these things rarely ever end up working out well." Nevertheless I wanted to meet him or at least write him a letter to see if I would get a reply.

So, late one afternoon I sat outside his nice house. I had debated at length about the contents of the handwritten letter I planned to either give him or post through his door. But as I sat there I wondered why I had never ever had a Christmas or Birthday card from him. And I wondered what he looked like and daydreamed about us perhaps getting close over time. I also wondered if he knew he'd sentenced us to a life of abject poverty when he left, and I wondered why he never wanted me or to know anything about me and why he had deserted us.

Being a child from a single parent family, you always long for a Dad, a better standard of living and above all, to see your Mum happy and free from the monotonous stresses caused by raising a family on your own and on the breadline. I wished that just once my Dad would reach out to me. I still wish for that, even to this day. Most of my life I have felt like an unwanted piece of trash, partly because of what my Dad did to me. I also held him responsible for the times when I was growing up and things were really tough. I could have really done with having a father. Unless you are from a single parent family all these questions are hard to answer. I guess it's probably similar to those people who are religious and wonder about meeting their maker.

My Dad was only steps away from where I was parked. As I sat outside his house, I read the letter I'd written one more time. Then I put it in the envelope and sealed it. While I was still agonising over what to do, I noticed someone was in one of the rooms at the front of the house. It looked like a teenage boy, He had a football shirt on and then sat down and switched the TV on. This could be my half-brother. I wondered what his name was? Another million questions ran through my head all at the same time.

Something inside of me wanted to knock on the door at that very moment and speak to him, even if I had to make up a silly excuse to do it. This really was a tipping point for me. The letter was in my hand, signed, sealed and in the envelope. And within 50 feet of my Dad's front door. And maybe a half-brother.

But then something clicked in my head. I burst into tears and started hitting the steering wheel repeatedly as every emotion I had ever had on the subject flowed out of me in a raging torrent. I found myself shouting, "Wanker, wanker, wanker." Then it came to me. I'm too good to be part of this piece of shit's life. I got the envelope that contained the letter I had toiled so hard over and ripped it to bits. Then I drove off.

That day certainly drew a line in the sand for me as I have hardly ever thought about him since. I love my Mum; she is and always will be both parents to me. And she deserves to be after bringing us up on her own. I have always looked up to my older brothers and seen them as role models. In the end I figured out that I had nothing to gain from meeting my Dad. As far I was concerned he had lost any right to know me – as far back as I could remember I had never seen or heard from him and I have never discovered why.

Poverty

The second thing I've wrestled with, all these years is the events that led up to an innocent 12-year-old boy feeling lost and suicidal at one point. I longed for Mum to meet someone: to try to make our family whole again, in the absence of my Dad. She had seen a few men on and off for short periods when I was a child, but for one reason or other things never really worked out. But when I was twelve she met someone called Dennis who had a son, Dan, who was in his late 20s, early 30s. They had their own house in Horndean. Dennis was a teacher and as far as I can remember Dan never worked.

After a few successful dates Mum introduced me to them. At first everything was really nice. Dennis was a fairly practical guy and was pretty interesting and Mum certainly seemed happy in his company. Well, certainly the happiest I had seen her for a good few years and that was important to me. Dan spoke a little oddly but seemed nice enough. I'm not sure if he had some kind of problem or if it was just a speech thing. But he did look a little odd, with his thick hair and eyebrows.

Whenever we went to their house, Dennis and my Mum seemed really happy. And Dan would be nothing but nice to me. For an older guy he seemed to love everything that I did and said he even watched the same cartoons and TV programmes as me. I could watch whatever I liked on the TV in his bedroom and he would bring me chocolate bars and crisps. He seemed like a real top guy. He would ask me all sorts of questions about school, my friends, how things were at home and about my Mum.

One day when we were on our own Dan said, "Let's play a little game of Hide and Seek." I hid in a wardrobe in his room but he locked me in and point blank refused to let me out saying, "I will only let you out when you do as you are told." I was screaming and kicking to get out but to no avail. So I said, "Ok, sure yeah, now let me out." When he opened the door I darted out. "What the hell was that all about?" But Dan just laughed and said, "It was just a bit of fun."

Over the coming months he started buying me things and I'm not just talking about chocolate bars. He bought me a stereo out of the blue from Asda in Waterlooville. He always used to offer to babysit for Mum so she could go out with Dennis. And he took a keen interest in my circle of friends. When I mentioned we were going swimming at Havant Leisure Centre he jumped at the chance to take us; even offering to pay for us. Quite frankly I was starting to find him creepier and creepier as he got deeper and deeper into our lives.

I used to like to go swimming as a child but I wasn't keen on going with Dan. I remember one day I went with Cotton and Dale and we walked all the way there. And it was quite a distance to Havant from where we lived, maybe seven or eight miles at a guess. After swimming we could not face the walk home. Cotton said: "You boys go and wait over there, I will sort some transport out." About ten minutes later he rode back on a BMX he had stolen and handed it to me. Ten minutes after that he came back with a racer for Dale, and then shortly after he came back with an almost brand new Peugeot racing bike for himself.

Basically Cotton used to sit in school messing about with bike combination locks and would work out how to pick them by pulling on them and turning the numbers at the same time. This was obviously a new skill he wanted to shown off so he had gone back to the Leisure Centre bike racks and simply stolen three bikes. I was really in two minds as to whether to walk home or ride this stolen bike and run the gauntlet with the police. I objected for about ten minutes but then jumped on the bike because I just wanted to get home. We took the country route home through Rowlands Castle and never had any problems with the police or anything. Dale took his bike home and I stashed Cotton's at my house so his parents would not ask any questions.

The next day we went for a cycle ride around Purbrook Heath. We went quickly down a really steep hill and Dale's bike had brake failure so he split off at the bottom of the road and went head first through a barbed wire fence. After we stopped laughing we looked at him holding his face and he had blood pouring all over him. There was a pretty nasty cut on his cheek that was 'L' shaped" and measured several inches. He also had a large flap of skin hanging down that he had to hold up the whole way home as we walked with the bikes. After we got back Cotton said he had a buyer for his bike. But it turned out that this older lad just stole it from him; he knew it was stolen so there was nothing he could do about it. Cotton was gutted but just said: "Shit happens," and shrugged his shoulders. Then he droned on about being a professional.

A few weeks later I took my stolen BMX to Waterlooville and put it down for literally thirty seconds and some asshole stole it. I had really liked this bike as well! Unfortunately, this was the way things went. So much stuff was 'acquired' you just had to accept that most things you owned were on a temporary basis. They had probably been acquired to start with and would be 'acquired' again.

The Reservation

Dale had left his bike on the Heath, as he had had to hold his face together on the way home. Although it was hidden in a bush it had also been acquired overnight. All three of our stolen rides had been stolen off us within two weeks. No wonder no one had anything nice.

I avoided swimming with Dan as much as possible but he still forced me into that cupboard several more times when our parents were out and locked me in it for what felt like hours. He seemed to get some kind of twisted enjoyment out of it. And when he let me out he used to say things like, "If you are a good boy and do what you are told, I will let you out." Then, when he let me out, he'd come over all friendly, saying, "Here is a nice chocolate bar and a cup of tea; that was fun wasn't it?" and put his arm around my shoulder. "Fancy going swimming again at the weekend or maybe I could come to yours?" Twelve years old or not, I knew this guy was freaky but I thought, maybe he is just a bit weird in some kind of mental illness or disability way.

I tried avoiding him at every opportunity but with our parents seeing each other, it was pretty difficult. He continued to buy me things and ask all sorts of questions about my life. I wasn't stupid and never trusted him. I tried to make sure my friends were with me as often as I could. They thought he was strange as well.

My Mum came home one day and said, "Martin I have some great news." She then went on to tell me that the four of us were going on a caravanning holiday in Devon. On the one hand this was great. Going on holiday was really exciting and one of those luxuries that proper families had. But on the other I would have to spend a week with Dan. But surely in a caravan the creep would be okay? It was hardly like I could refuse as it was the happiest I had seen my Mum in quite some time. And at twelve I knew I could never stay on my own at home for a week, even if I could look after myself.

We all took the train to Weston-super-Mare and then a taxi to a caravan park by the sea. It was a really nice place although the caravan was pretty cramped. The night we arrived I managed to give Dan the slip and went for a nice long walk down a sandy beach in my bare feet. I love the feel of sand between my toes. It is one of life's little pleasures. I remember the crickets singing in the long grass as I walked back to the caravan. The wind had picked up a little and I started to feel the sprinkle of warm rain. Everyone asked where I'd been but other than that it was an uneventful night. We went to the caravan park social centre for dinner and then all went to bed.

The next day we all went out on an open top bus. Then Dennis and my Mum decided to nip out for a walk while I was stuck with Dan watching a bit of TV. I decided I needed a shower. But to my absolute horror, as I was washing my hair Dan started rubbing soap on my shoulders and was stark naked next to me. "I couldn't get the water the right temperature earlier when I showered, so thought I would join you." The image of him standing there, with everything hanging out, haunts me to this day. Putting each and every word of this, on the page, is a very uncomfortable thing to do even now.

I think I was frozen in shock and the small shower only had one way in or out so I found myself completely stuck. I glared at him and started thumping and kicking as I tried to get past him. After a struggle I managed to wriggle free and made my way into the caravan screaming and shouting. "You are a freak." He just replied, "Why? I was only helping you take a shower." I then said I was telling but he said, "Go on then but our parents won't believe you. And it will split them up and make them unhappy."

As soon as the opportunity presented itself I put on my shorts and T-shirt and made a run for it along the beach. I stopped after I could run no further and tried to get my head together. What on earth had just happened? What was I going to do and what would I say to my Mum? I had so many thoughts going around in my head but then it became crystal clear. All these chocolate bars, trips to the swimming pool and gifts had been leading up to this moment for him.

I didn't hear the expression 'grooming' or the word paedophile until about three or four years later but as soon as I did, I knew what they were. And I immediately thought of this low life piece of shit called Dan. I decided in my own little mind not to tell my Mum because maybe he was right and she wouldn't believe me. But I also decided I couldn't stay there a day longer with that freak. When I got back I told my Mum I was going home with or without her as I hated it here and cried non-stop until she agreed to take me home. Dennis and Dan stayed for the remainder of the holiday.

That holiday ended up causing so much resentment between our parents. Unfortunately, because my Mum left with me, her and Dennis split up not long afterwards. So there was no need for me to say anything, other than telling her to leave him again and again. I am a really placid guy but I have often thought about what I would ever do or say to Dan if I were to see him again. The thought of him, and what he was trying to do to me, a small innocent boy, repels me to the pit of my stomach even now.

Even to this day I really struggle with going away on holiday and try to avoid them at all costs. I know it is a direct result of what happened to me on this one. I know things could have turned out a whole lot worse and other people have suffered terrible torment as children at the hands of adults. And I can see how these low lives can so easily manipulate children. Life in my opinion has always been about keeping things in perspective; if it's raining, it could be freezing cold, and if it's freezing cold it could be snowing. If it's snowing and you are cold, it could be windy and so on.

For me personally it was extremely hard to write about this. I struggle to even think about the events that took place. Most of the time, they are locked away, at the back of my mind, in the hope that someday they will vanish. But after about thirty years these memories still haunt me so I have chosen to bare all; in the hope that by talking about them, somehow I will be freed. Even my closest family will be surprised by what I have written. But I beg anyone close to me never to discuss any of this with me. These words are my own form of some sort of closure.

The Reservation

Chapter Four
A Leap of Faith

It was the summer of 1988 and there wasn't much to do on the Reservation during those long, hot days. We longed to go swimming. If you felt really adventurous you could walk all the way to Hilsea and go to the Lido. It is an outdoor Art Deco style swimming pool and although it was beginning to show its age, it was still fantastic and was one of the locations for the 70s film Tommy.

It was probably a walk of around four or five miles each way. Cotton would regularly scale the Lido fence and either steal trainers or clothes and hop back over and run off. Usually we'd head down there just as they were closing. The guards used to stand there all day, keeping an eye on the crowd gathered outside the fences. They knew fully well that the moment they left, the pool would be invaded. We had many a great swim there in the evenings, although the locals could get a bit rough in the water. If you crossed their path they would try to drown you!

But most of the time we sent swimming closer to home. Next to my school was another school called Crookhorn and was only a fifteen minutes' walk from home. One of us would bring a ghetto blaster and we would normally stop for a little breakdance on the way. We'd stop on a street corner and do our stuff to the sounds of Electro 9 or Roxanne Shante. Batteries were normally in short supply so we used to put them in the oven for a bit before leaving, to get the last bit of juice out of them. But normally breakdancing was limited. The tapes used up a lot of power so volume was kept low to save juice but at least the radio passed the time.

Crookhorn pool was really nice but it was fairly challenging to get to. Firstly, you had to scale a couple of chain fences and the last one was around eight feet tall. And we had to make a human chain to pass the ghetto blaster over. Unfortunately, you'd end up getting covered in vandal proof paint. This truly awful invention never stopped you but the grey goo would stick to your one and only prized shell suit and never come off. I guess someone somewhere had the brainwave that destroying an Adidas shell suit would act as a deterrent. I guess that was what it was meant to do but to me, ruining shell suits was a criminal act in those days. In the end we used to put the suits on inside out so at least they never looked bad on the outside.

Now once you'd done Prison Break in reverse to get to the pool, you could enjoy the cool water and have a paddle. That was until the caretaker shouted at you or the police turned up and you made a run for it.

Next to the deep end was a flat-roofed building that used to have classrooms in it. I remember it being pretty high and a fair distance from the actual pool. We used to brag that we would somehow climb onto the top of this building and make the leap of faith into the water down below. One day I finally got talked into it. I remember climbing up a drainpipe that was smothered in vandal proof paint I only had shorts on so was quickly covered in the stuff. Great big clumps were clinging to my near-naked body and as I pulled away, quite a bit of body hair was ripped off. After much struggling I reached the flat roof but the edge nearest the pool had barbed wire across. This was obviously to deter any would-be idiots from attempting to kill themselves by jumping into the pool. Gingerly I walked across the pea-shingled roof towards the edge. The stones were digging into my soft feet as I peered over. Gee, it really did look like a killer jump. It was one of those terrible peer pressure moments. Everyone tells you to, "Do it, you'll be fine," but you're really only doing it for their amusement and in the hope of seeing you go splat on the concrete below.

After what seemed like an eternity I came to my senses. I must have been mad to even think of doing it. But a few of the kids could see I was having doubts so had ripped the drainpipe off the wall. I was trapped. Then they started throwing various objects at me, including my trainers and even stones. I was left with no choice; I was going to have to jump. I put my trainers on and took one last look from behind the barbed wire. If I jumped too late, I'd get tangled up in the barbed wire, trip and fall to my death on the concrete below. Jump too early, you might avoid the barbed wire but fall short of the pool and again hit the concrete. And even if I did clear the barbed wire and landed in the deepest part of the pool, I'd probably break something.

This really was an absolutely stupid thing to do. My malnourished, stick thin body would shatter into a million pieces if anything went wrong. In a split second I decided to go for it. I ran at top speed across the flat roof, jumped the row of barbed wire and flew like a bird. It was almost like being in a car crash. Everything slowed down as my senses heightened and for a moment I appreciated the craziness of what I was doing. I decided that win or lose; I would give it my best shot. So as I somersaulted through the air, I pulled myself into a small ball and prepared for the worst.

I was expecting to feel the hard concrete and the pain of crushed bones but instead I felt cold water going up my nostrils and entering my gasping mouth. I slowed down and came to a standstill and then gently bounced off the bottom of the pool. As I started to float upwards I could hear the sound of jubilant screaming and applause. Not only had I done it but I'd lived to tell the tale. And I'd managed to set a new standard among my friends of idiotic bravery. This day sticks in my mind because it was the day that the boy became a man, in terms of self-esteem.

Over the coming months most of my friends failed to take the challenge, despite the drainpipe being fixed. Feeling the pressure to jump, they would suggest other places to swim. As word got round of my achievement, I heard rumours that several people from the Reservation broke their legs and nearly died attempting this jump. I don't know if any of those rumours were actually true but to this day that jump still horrifies me. But it gave me strength and helped me overcome some of my inner fears.

Wes was a latecomer to our group. He was a bit too clever and lived off the Reservation. His parents were a bit over-protective and his Mum was bordering on terrifying. We had been friends for a few years. Wes was thoughtful and turned out to be really funny. Unfortunately, his parents dressed him like something out of The Brady Bunch so he lacked any kind of style. We nicknamed him 'Wes the Steg'.

I remember once Fizz and I were rummaging through his wardrobe while he was eating his dinner. We found a raincoat with 'WES' written in huge letters across it. Fizz put it on along with some of his other funky clothes but when Wes came back up he went mental. He didn't see the funny side at all. He was in such a rage that he started throwing his arms around and kicking us so hard that we had to flee.

Wes was the first person I knew with his own computer; his Amiga was awesome. We used to go to his house and play games on it for hours. Now this guy was bright and could do almost anything with a computer. If the movie Weird Science was actually possible it would have been Wes who made the girl. We all had a lot of respect for his technical ability. This was the guy who, a few years later showed me the internet and said: "This will be massive." And he was also the first person to show me porn online. Wes really loved his porn. We all did. As a group we had tons of porn mags that we used to share. They'd either been shoplifted by Cotton or stolen from Jones' Dad.

Wes had learned how to get his fix online years before it became the norm. He was a computer whiz. While the rest of us were looking at disgusting, borrowed magazines with pages stuck together that failed to open without ripping, Wes was living the dream. Thanks to his computer, he had an endless supply of porn on tap. Wes lived quite a distance from the Reservation and had a high IQ. So he was one of those people who floated in and out of our circle of friends.

The Reservation

In the third year I remember having a beach party on Hayling sand dunes with some of the other guys. Hayling sand dunes was a reasonably nice party venue. Although you had to walk for about a mile from the car park and the dunes were more like scrubland and covered in thick vegetation. Everyone got an invite but as you would expect, hardly anyone from school came for two reasons. Firstly, who on earth cared about us losers? And secondly the weather was terrible. The sky was grey and it was windy and rainy on and off all night. But we managed to get smashed on cheap beer, Gut Wrench and a bottle of vodka.

Wes was absolutely wrecked, I mean so wrecked he kept trying to walk into the sea with his arms raised looking like Christ on the cross. The tide around here had claimed many an innocent person. It was brutal and well known for being merciless. As a matter of safety we decided to tie Wes to one of the bushes to stop him roaming off and drowning. He had this really awful green and grey skiing jacket with a big 'V' on the front and back that everyone detested. This jacket had miraculously survived many attempts to destroy it.

All of us had Zippo lighters along with a small can of lighter fluid to refill their lighter; or, all too often, take a sniff. I have no idea who started it but it became a bit of a joke to squirt lighter fluid on each other and set light to it. This soon became known as 'flicksies'. They'd always squirt the fluid on your back and then someone would light it by flicking matches at it from a distance. You were blissfully unaware until everyone started laughing; or you felt the flames or could smell the smoke. When stoned this was immensely funny.

A Leap of Faith

The jacket survived 'flicksies" several times after lighter fluid was thrown on it and lit matches had been flicked on it, yet there was only minor damage. One thing was for sure, everyone hated the bloody thing. But this jacket was indestructible. We had tried to steal it, burn it and rip it to bits but it proved difficult because the jacket never left his side.

While Wes was tied to the bush and out cold, Fizz started to piss on him. That night everyone used him as a toilet and thought it was hilarious. We really enjoyed the thought of him waking up, stinking of piss and would finally throw away that bloody jacket. I have to say everyone was pleased it wasn't them being used as a urinal. After a terrible night's sleep, with people throwing up everywhere and the wind and rain freezing you to the bone, the sun finally came up. So we decided to wake Wes up and start the long walk to the bus stop. But he just got up and said he was starving and still feeling sick. He never even noticed that he had been used all night as a public urinal.

We pooled all the money we had and bought a croissant each and stole some milk from a doorstep to help with the hangovers until the bus came. Unsurprisingly, every time Wes sat next to someone they moved; I guess he thought it was because he had been so sick. He never did notice the jacket's smell or, to my knowledge, ever washed it. His parents must have thought they had a stray tom cat at home or something. That jacket was minging but it refused to die. It was legendary but never left Wes' side. It was like Charlie Brown's blanket.

Finally, six months or so later, Cotton set fire to the jacket while doing 'flicksies'. He successfully managed to flick a match directly into the folded back hood from about 5 feet away. Only moments earlier he had secretly squirted the hood with Zippo lighter fuel while walking behind Wes. As it started burning we looked at each other in amazement; were we about to get shot of it at last? Suddenly Wes noticed the flames and smoke and quickly removed his jacket to avoid losing his hair. He threw it on the floor and started stamping on it. By now we were laughing but to Wes' annoyance the flames weren't going out, despite all the stamping. We watched in awe as the jacket continued to burn. It was like witnessing some Viking burial at sea.

Wes was furious, I mean absolutely furious. Flicksies with matches and lighter fluid had been on a sabbatical for a good while, because no one could replace their clothes and it was winter. And although we'd all been set on fire at some point, you could see how angry Wes was. But over the years we all grew really fond of Wes. He was really funny especially while smoking pot; raving and talking endlessly about porn while stoned.

A few years later, in 1992, Wes had done himself proud. He had somehow been given the job as manager of a computer shop in Havant. It was located in a 1970s looking precinct next to the entrance to the railway station. He was really pleased; it was a great job and came with its own flat above the shop. I mean seriously, this guy was always going to do well. A manager's job at such a young age and his own flat. Us mortals could only dream of such things. Wes picked the keys up and asked us if we wanted to look at the flat. We all piled in and it was really nice by our standards. We immediately set about 'skinning up' and sticking a rave tape on. Over the next few hours we became more and more stoned and someone pinned up a Jamaican flag over the fireplace. Then we set about stomping up and down to the enticing beat of the sweet rave music coming out of the stereo. As Wes got more wasted he lost control and the music got louder and louder. We were screaming out the windows at girls in the precinct and telling them to come on up.

The neighbours kept coming round but their pleas for silence fell on deaf ears. Then I looked up and saw someone I didn't recognise in the lounge. He had clearly let himself in as he had the keys in his hand. He was red in the face and screaming and looked like he was going to have a cardiac. Everyone continued dancing and just laughed at him until he kicked the stereo over and then, in a really posh but frustrated voice, he screamed, "Where is Wesley?" I mean who the hell was that? Oh, he must mean Wes. He's the one passed out on the sofa, under the massive Jamaican Cannabis flag that had just been pinned on the wall.

Someone shook Wes into consciousness and as he woke up he looked like he'd seen a ghost. The colour quickly drained from his cheeks and you could see he was completely smashed. But something deep inside was trying to shock him into a conscious state. After some more screaming it turned out that the very frustrated gentleman was in fact Wes' boss and he owned the shop... and the flat. He had been called out because we had been jumping so much we'd set the shop alarm off. He'd then been alerted that there was the party of all parties going on upstairs.

You could see he was less than impressed with his new manager's circle of friends, taste in music and obvious passion for a bit of puff. Wes was fired on the spot without ever starting work in the shop. He denied emphatically that he had been smoking pot but I think maybe the flag and the fact he looked like a Zombie might have given the game away. No end of sweet-talking by Wes was going to keep his job or stop us from being thrown out, there and then. I think it was probably character building for him in the long run. This geeky guy had learnt at last how to let his hair down. And in the end he laughed about it all like a real sport.

Chapter Five
Port Road

I was 15-years-old and although not old enough to ride a moped, my Mum used to lend me hers on the odd occasion, or I would 'borrow' the keys when she was home in the evening. Several of us had mopeds because a few of my friends were a little older than me. We could get away from the Reservation and often went to Swain's house in Port Road in Cosham. His Dad had met a woman called Alison and was very rarely at home, so it made an ideal hang out. We used to spend countless hours there smoking 'blow' and getting alcohol from the local corner shop, because Swain could easily get served there.

As the evenings wore on, we would get louder and louder as we played rave music at increasingly loud levels. The anti-social behaviour going on at this house was unbelievable. People were screaming and shouting all night and the music was so loud that the neighbours would bang on the door in the middle of the night. But no one could hear them, so their calls for help generally went unanswered. One neighbour apparently changed her bedroom so she could try to get some sleep. Despite being elderly and partially deaf, the relentless thud of the bass was too much even for her to take. Another neighbour used to frantically bang the wall in the early hours. But instead of turning the music down, we turned the speakers around and turned it up. Simultaneously, with each beat, we all used to stand with our backs to the wall, on one leg. Then we'd thump the wall with the other foot, to the beat of the music, until the house shook.

My school friend Gal started spending more and more time over at Swain's. And while stoned they used to obsess about dealing drugs or Gal used to say he could make Speed, because his Dad was a professor of chemistry. He claimed he was going to make some, fill a barrel and bury the drugs at a secret location. Gal was a fairly small blonde kid and lived off the Reservation in a private house. He always seemed to have very good prospects at school. Academically he was fairly bright and took great pride in looking after anything he ever owned.

Looking back this was probably the tipping point in Gal' s life. He went from being a good child and a great student with a promising future, to a drug dealer in about six months flat. He decided that he admired drugs so much that he was going to deal Speed. He used to buy it from some ravers on the top of Portsdown Hill. They used to drive an old red Yugo so were known as the 'Yugo Boys'. Now if you don't know what a Yugo is, it was a car made in the former Eastern Bloc. Gal then used to cut the stuff with anything he could lay his hands on. But more often than not it was glucose from the chemist or baking soda. He used to sit at Swain's, cutting it all up and I can still vividly remember Swain standing over him, bouncing about on the spot, rattling his hands in his pockets. He couldn't contain his excitement when he saw all the white stuff laid out on the table. Over the next few years the two of them became very close, experimenting with anything they could lay their hands on. I would often see Gal consuming eight or ten wraps of speed at a time and Swain begging for a few wraps, just like a little puppy, begging for scraps of food from his master's table.

Port Road descended into a really noisy doss house and drug den for us Reservation lads. We used to spend hour after hour there smoking pot, getting pissed and listening to loud rave music. It goes without saying that it was just a question of time until the police raided the place, especially as the police station was only about five minutes down the road and everyone that Gal 'served up' used to blatantly get gear off him at the front door. Deals were done in broad daylight. So one morning the house was finally raided by the police. We opened the door and they ran through the house and started searching it. The police patted down all the rave flyers taped on the wall and began questioning everyone. Swain's Dad was a solicitor but fortunately was not at home that day but he was clearly not impressed when he found out.

Although the police found drug-taking paraphernalia they didn't find any drugs. Gal had his stash hidden under the shed and they never looked in the garden. After Swain's Dad got wind of some of the problems at home, he started being around more, along with his girlfriend Alison. We couldn't stand her – and she hated us. In return, Swain and his little brother set about making her life hell. Alison banished us all to the shed. We thought it was quite cool but she would spoil it by randomly coming out and telling us off for something or other. One day we were out there and she literally kicked the door down, screaming her head off.

When Alison moved in with Swain's Dad she put all her

valuables in the loft. One day, on the walk home from the train station, she noticed all her prized possessions for sale in the local pawnbroker's. The Swain kids had been selling them to buy dope and any other drugs they could get their hands on; her family heirlooms had been ravaged and now sold. As she stood there screaming at the two of them, we were all so stoned, surrounded by a thick cloud of smoke, that we just laughed as she kicked and punched them. At the time this seemed funny, but looking back at this sort of thing now, I cringe – and I'm really not proud of how we behaved.

We were told to get out of the shed so we decided to go to Hilsea Lines. We had Scabby Jake with us. He was another good friend of Swain's and was a very small lad with dark hair who fancied himself as a bit of an East End gangster, as he was originally from London. He wore the same top for years, seven days a week. It was affectionately known as 'The Frog Top' as it had lines and lines of little frogs on it, in an Egyptian sort of pattern, and was green.

Scabby Jake was a regular tagger; wherever he went he used to take an aerosol can out of his pocket and spray his tag. On the way to the Lines we stopped off at Les Smith, a car shop in Cosham, and Scabby Jake stole a variety of cans of paint. After walking through the Lines we ended up in a very narrow and dark Victorian railway tunnel. After Scabby Jake sprayed the outline of design on the wall, everyone got to work spraying it.

But after about ten minutes we heard a freight train coming and everything started to rumble and shake. As it got closer and closer, Scabby Jake shouted, "Quick, get against the wall," so we all stood with our backs flat against the wall. I can't tell you how scared

I was; my mouth was dry and every hair on my body stood on end and tingled with a mixture of fear and anticipation. I thought about running to the end of the tunnel but there was no time. And the train would probably hit me. As the earth beneath my feet shook harder and harder and the wall I was stood against started vibrating, I could see the lights on the front of the train coming towards me. They were brightly glowing in the dark tunnel.

As the train went past me I screamed, as I was so scared; it was literally inches away from me. It felt like the vacuum was sucking the air out of my lungs and my hair was being pulled towards it by the backdraft created by the train. Then, as if in a moment of madness, I realised that I was going to live and started laughing uncontrollably. I found it really exciting. After the train passed, we finished off the rather poor looking graffiti we'd been working on and walked out of the tunnel in a surprisingly jovial manner. Swain had found a long bar next to the train track and was dragging it along behind him. Then we heard another train coming. "Run," laughed Swain as he threw the metal bar onto the tracks and we all fled to a safe distance.

All of a sudden there was a loud screeching sound and we could see huge sparks coming from the train's undercarriage. The sparks lit up the train and it looked like a sparkler on Guy Fawke's Night. The train appeared to be in a lot of trouble and the driver was trying to perform an emergency stop to avoid a possible derailment. We could hear the passengers screaming at the tops of their voices and the loud high pitched whine of the brakes as the train came to an abrupt stop. Two rail workers got off the train and had a look underneath. Then they spotted us and chased us into the thick woodland by the track, where we quickly lost them.

A few weeks later we were all at Port Road smoking pot and decided to go and buy some chips as we all had the 'munchies'. We were sat on a bench on the opposite side of the road to the 'chippy', laughing and joking. It was one of those really nice, hot summer days with a beautiful blue sky. People were enjoying the weather and it almost looked like a resort somewhere on the continent. We were sitting next to a phone box opposite Peacocks the department store in Cosham High Street. In a stoned state Swain went into the phone box and started messing around. Before we knew it he had called the phone number displayed on the front of the Peacocks store. And in an Irish accent said, "There's a bomb in your shop. I am giving you 5 minutes to evacuate." Then he calmly walked out of the phone box and sat back on the wall. Moments later people came running out of the shop screaming and police from the station about 200 yards away started running down the road. Police cars pulled up and it was a hive of activity as the bewildered customers were escorted from the shop and a cordon set up.

One of the police asked us, "Do you know anything about this?" as we were all hanging around laughing, instead of running away like everybody else. We just said, "No, of course not," and merrily walked back to Port Road to finish our chips.

Back on the Reservation the evenings passed in a never-ending cycle of 'trundling' around the estate. Some nights we used to walk miles avoiding the people who caused us problems and having a bit of fun or chatting to the local girls.

I can remember Cotton knocking on his girlfriend's door one night with a couple of us. Her Mother came to the door and said, "I will get her," and yelled her name and then walked off. The next minute someone had squirted lighter fuel on the back of Cotton's coat and set fire to him. He stood there blissfully unaware he was slowly burning, eagerly waiting for her. We all took a few steps back, trying to stop ourselves from laughing. By the time she came to the door, Cotton had smoke and flames coming from the back of him. His girlfriend screamed, "Fuck me, you're on fire." We all started rolling about laughing as he quickly took his jacket off and stamped on it. I can only imagine what the poor girl thought seeing him in the dark like that. Waiting for her, with a pleasant smile on his face, as the lighter fluid burnt into his back, blissfully unaware of the flames behind him. He must have looked like something from a dream or the Devil himself! After everyone complained about their clothes being set on fire we stopped and started setting post-boxes on fire instead. We were stoned and had run for our lives when the odd policeman chased us. This provided a bit of light entertainment when we had nothing else to do.

Sometimes Cotton would commit a minor burglary and steal some alcohol for us all but I hated robbery. I was an honest kid with a strong moral compass; well in Reservation terms anyway, so I always left them to it. I never wanted to be involved or associated with anything like that. Cotton would get himself the odd thing to sell or barter with. He would often turn up at your door with an electric razor or something like that, that had no mains lead. Or those plug-in commercial hair trimmers, that were clearly stolen from the local barbers. But seriously, he was a terrible thief who got caught far too often. Cotton was one of the thickest criminal minds around locally. He used to do a fair bit of opportunistic petty crime but he rarely ever thought anything through.

On the way home from school he used to walk past another school in Purbrook. He burgled it three days running at exactly the same time and was baffled when the police were waiting for him on the third day. Like a scene out of a film, I believe he was apprehended running across the roof with the school sun dial on him, trying to hold on to another load of useless items he hoped to sell. In school he often had bits of 'vandal proof' paint stuck to the lower part of his jumper. He had obviously been stretching his arms to break in to somewhere or other. As a small group of friends we were growing ever closer and were sharing so many experiences together. In those years I don't think I had ever been so close to a group of people in my entire life. We all had problems, we all had our differences, but we all shared a common bond that you could only find when you experienced so much together. We more often than not tried to look out for each other but like in any other group, there were always little rifts between us.

Chapter Six
Sweet Sixteen

It was my last year at school and I had fallen absolutely and madly in love with a girl called Mandy about a year before. She had long, blonde hair and wonderful eyes and a smile that lit up her face. I had met Mandy at a school disco and was immediately attracted to her. She was wearing a black and silver mini skirt with black tights that showed off her lovely long legs and a pair of black high heels with a silver bow and a flower on. In 80s terms she was smoking hot. After having a slow dance with her I said, "Hey tasty chick, wanna go out with me?" I mean seriously, what the hell had just come out of my mouth? Of all the things I could have said, why that? It was so cringe worthy. But to my astonishment she said yes!

Over the coming months we began to get very close and I would call her every night from the local phone box and spend as much time as I could with her at school. Mandy was a very clever girl from a good family in Clanfield. She had good grades and studied really hard. I, on the other hand, was a bit rough by comparison; well at least on the outside. Her parents were very strict. I think it was a case of them trying to hold onto their little daughter.

Anyway, I ended up getting into a little bit of bother at school. Basically Cotton and Dale had decided to break into the sixth form locker room one night and steal a load of stuff. I would never participate in any acts like that as Cotton normally got caught and I didn't agree with stealing. But somehow I got dragged into it by receiving stolen goods in the shape of a tennis racket that I purchased from Cotton. Okay on probability I guessed it was stolen but he never said and I never asked. It was around the same time as Swain and Scabby Jake decided to break in and steal all the school motorbikes that were used for a Learn to Ride programme in the playground so the timing could not have been much worse as the school was trying to crack down on this new crime wave.

Our small group of friends had certainly been in the thick of it lately. Cotton had blabbed that it was him who had broken into the locker room; everything he stole he blabbed about and got caught for, it was always the same. And Scabby Jake and Swain had been caught riding the school's Yamaha RD 50 up and down the back of Portsdown Hill. They were caught red handed. There had often been banter about stealing the school motorbikes but until then that was all it had been. Scabby Jake used to say, "I bet that RD well flies, it's never been out of first gear." Unlike Cotton, they had kept it very quiet until they were caught by the police and held to account by the school.

We were all suspended in the space of about a week for all these things. I guess it was just bad timing but these things happen. When I returned to school our Year Head, Mr Lewis, called me into his office and explained I had been silly buying the tennis racket, knowing it was stolen. Now I agree I guessed it was stolen but how else was I going to afford to buy it? Practically everything you bought on the Reservation was acquired. You took your turn buying something stolen, and then something was stolen from you. It was just the way things worked. The natural process of sharing and survival of the fittest all came into play.

Mr Lewis then told me we were all being split up but I was surprised when he gave me the choice of which class I could be put into. I chose Mandy's in a heartbeat. He knew why, because all the teachers thought we were very cute together, so warmly smiled at me. I think he thought that as Mandy was a good girl, she would be a calming influence on me. Mr Lewis knew I was from a deprived family and he knew I had been bullied because he had got involved after the education welfare officer visited my Mum and I had to explain my problems in school. But he also knew I was generally a good kid; maybe he spotted some potential in me or maybe he was just doing his job. I will never know.

But life at my school was never dull. In an enterprising way we all used to trade items for food or money and often these too were acquired. But I had certainly started the trading trend while I was in the first year. Keeping yourself afloat was of paramount importance as you were growing up on the Reservation. I figured out that business was to be my great redeemer.

I started a car cleaning round with a friend of mine called Jeff Walker. We would both cycle all over the place on our BMXs and knock on doors all day for business. He was a top kid. He lived in a road nearby and had always been really friendly towards me. He was fairly tall and blonde and was absolutely BMX crazy. I can remember even as a small child sitting on the kerb outside his house and discussing business names and ways to get the money rolling in. We did all the right things even as children. We started with a borrowed bucket and sponge and then reinvested the proceeds into a nice Halford's set so we looked even more professional. We then cornered the market by cleaning work vans at a local intruder alarms depot in Purbrook. The lesson here is if you want something in life enough, even at an early age, you can get it. If you get off your ass, you can make things happen.

With my cut of the car cleaning proceeds I decided to expand my business empire into the classroom. I'd managed to raise enough money to take a trip to a local, run-down wholesale shop in a local town called Cowplain. Here, I spent the money on fizz-bombs and Wham bars, which I proceeded to peddle from my desk. To my delight, I sold out within a few days and made quite a healthy profit. Over the coming months I had earned quite a reputation as being the class shop. My classmates could see good money exchanging hands as a consequence so new trading outlets opened every day in our classroom. It got to the stage where you could acquire almost anything you needed from one pupil or another, vended from an open desk.

It was like a bear pit where stocks and shares are traded because as the bell went, all the desks closed and trading immediately ceased just as the Form Tutor would walk in. Trading commenced again as the bell rang at break time and at the end of the day. It put the Form Tutor and the school in an odd position. Instead of the children playing marbles or football at break times the kids were up to something, but what? I can remember two teachers staring through the window of our wooden hut that was our Form Room and wondering exactly what was going on. And what they could do about it.

It seemed that the classroom trading competition spilt the

beans. Soon one of those teachers dragged me out of registration by the ear and spent a great deal of time discussing the morals of depriving my classmates of their lunch money. I tried to explain that I was providing a valuable service by supplying sweet goods before the school canteen was open, and that this was a great lesson in enterprise. But I was told in, no uncertain terms, that I was going to be watched very closely and could be suspended if I was caught again.

Despite this I continued with a scaled down operation. My little side line – selling sweets at school – went well for a while, but eventually things started to go wrong. We began to run short of food at home and, over the period of a few weeks, I was forced to eat my stock to stave off the hunger. This not only made me feel sick, but also taught me a valuable lesson: never sell food or drink because, when times are hard, you're likely to devour it all!

In the years that followed, I often sat in school distracted by thoughts of running multi-million pound companies and driving around in Porsches or Ferraris.

One week just before I was thirteen, most of the pupils from school had gone on a foreign school trip for a week to Italy. Only about twenty or so of us remained behind; mainly the locals from the Reservation who couldn't afford to go and those who had been banned from travelling with the school (I was in the former group, I hasten to add).

For once, the teacher decided not to give us a hard time for that week and instead set us an exciting exercise. Each of us was to start a small business venture and the results would be assessed at the end of that week. This was the chance I had been waiting for and I sat for hours thinking about what I could do. That evening my Mum took me to a local auction and we bought £5 worth of jewellery. This mix of 1980s earrings and fake diamond rings was, of course, complete junk. Nevertheless, I lovingly washed and polished every last piece in preparation for the project. Over the next week, I watched with delight as the first and second year girls trotted dutifully over with their lunch money and handed it over in exchange for cheap accessories. Mine quickly became the most successful business of the class. I sold every item of jewellery. My closest competition was someone else in my year called Mike. He was from a comfortable background, was quite tall, with long, dark hair, played tennis and was heavily into sport. He had started a dating agency and it was a very, very close rival to my junk jewellery business. So close in fact, that for a small time I really did think it would make more money than mine. It had come to light that it was his tennis racket that I had bought, and he had even gone out with Mandy before me so it could not have been a more embarrassing situation to find myself in.

As the competition entered the last two days of the week, I changed tack to get better revenue. I got out of bed earlier in the morning to extend the selling time before school started. This ensured two things that contributed to my success. Firstly, it gave me another hour of selling time in the mornings and secondly it meant that I could deprive people of their money before Mike had a chance. I went on to build and run the most profitable business that week in school.

I was delighted by this achievement, along with the more dubious honour of being personally responsible for half the kids either getting detention or having their property seized by unimpressed teachers. I gave my Mum her original stake back and with the remainder of the money, my friends and I decided to purchase as much Kestrel Super-Strength as we could afford. By the end of our drinking session, my friends had to drag me home where they unceremoniously dumped me outside the front door, rang the bell and then legged it. My Mum opened the door to find me being sick all over the doorstep. This episode taught me two valuable lessons: firstly, if you can make money then you can have a good time. Secondly, lay off the Super-Strength on a school night when you are only thirteen.

Another funny memory from my school years was the sale of bikes that I used to salvage from the local dump at the weekend. I remember someone in my pottery class called Darren Jones. Darren was putting a handle on a pot he was making when he mentioned that his Mum had given him £15 to buy a BMX bike.

I gently put my arm around his shoulder, as I told him about a lovely BMX that I was selling. I described all the features and told him how much money he could save on his bus fare. He nodded his head as he excitedly agreed to buy it. I took a £5 deposit and promised to deliver the bike the next Tuesday after he had paid the rest of the balance. I didn't have a bike and it was Friday afternoon. I went to the dump at the weekend and searched for hours for old bits that could be used to build a gleaming bike that would be Darren's pride and joy. I ended up with a rusty painted pink frame and two odd buckled wheels and a few other parts.

I spent the next few days putting them together and trying to get it all working. It looked very odd, a cross between a BMX and a Shopper bike. I then decided that to smarten it up, it would have to be sprayed if I had any chance of passing it off as anything close to what I had sold him. I had spent the money that he had already paid me on one thing or another so I couldn't afford the spray paint. As I rummaged through the shed I found a tin of 'Signal Green' and a tin of 'White non-drip gloss'.

As fast as you can say abracadabra, I had ruined every piece of clothing I was wearing and had paint everywhere, as the only brush I could find was rock solid. I started off by painting the wheels and spokes white. The rust kept showing through so I had to put it on real thick. I then dipped the white paint brush in the 'Signal Green' paint and unsurprisingly, I ended up with a very odd looking runny kind of finish that started white and went bright green the more I painted it.

I let the bike dry for a day then took it into school. On the way in everyone was laughing at me. I parked it with all the other bikes then Darren came running over to collect it. Well the look on his face was indescribable as he looked shocked and horrified by this monstrosity he had purchased from me. It was the ugliest and worst bike I have ever seen. Looking back on it my eyes still fill with water as I laugh when I think about it. Darren had a bit of a stutter when he was under pressure so all I can remember is him managing to say, "M…MMMM…Martin," as the bell went off.

I hid for the rest of the day, dodging Darren in our shared lessons. After school I crept around the back of the Maths and Science block to see him cycling the bright green wreck along the road leading to his home, stopping every now and then to put the chain back on. I never saw him ride the bike again but I expect I know the fate of it.

Sweet Sixteen

Imagine what his Mum must have thought when she saw this green blob turn up at the house.

School was never dull. One time a girl called Jane and her brother Peter acquired several small, brown cardboard boxes of live WWII bullets they had found in their Grandad's loft. They came in dark brown boxes each containing twenty bullets and they became popular collectables for a while at school. These were live rounds - .22 and .33 calibre. The smaller ones looked like they were most likely for a pistol and the larger .33 ones for some kind of rifle or possibly a machine gun - yet we then set about taking them to bits. It was absolute madness looking back on it. We worked out that you could either twist the tops off the .22 ones with a pair of pliers or simply insert the tips into a large zip and bend them until the top came off.

At lunchtime we used to sit in our smoking spot in the woods taking them to bits. The small ones used to be filled with a black, granular gun powder and interestingly enough, we discovered that the larger ones were filled with spaghetti-like strands of gunpowder. So we mixed it together with Blue Tack, stuck it to some trees in the woods and set it on fire. As kids this kind of stuff was exciting to play with but the whole mixing it with Blue Tack was a bit of an anti-climax as it just fizzled on the tree. I'm not sure what we expected it to do though in all honesty.

Everything seemed just fine on the munitions front. Jane and Peter would bring a box of bullets into school, we'd get some from them and enjoy taking them to bits. That was until one day I was sat in the Language Lab, prodding a compass into the bottom of a .22 round; I had just taken the top off and poured the black powder out thinking it was safe. Suddenly there was a massive bang, which literally scared me to death, and a cloud of black smoke wafted upwards. Fortunately, the teacher, Mr Coote, could never control a class, so when he asked, "What was that?" there was already so much noise and disruption, no one said anything and he left it at that. It turns out that I had stabbed the starter cap in the bottom of the bullet and it had gone off. Looking back on it I'm pleased it was a round I had already taken to bits. But it did prove to me that these things were very much live and kicking so we needed to take care with them.

However, later that day I was literally dragged out of class, by my ear, by Mr Lewis. He got me in his office and started screaming at me about bullets that someone from a neighbouring school had been caught with. Basically I had swapped some for cigarettes with this guy called Graham, who lived near me, and he had been caught in school with them. Seriously, it was not really the sort of thing you should be boasting about in school, but then again I couldn't talk. I had showed him the bullets and swapped some. Within a matter of minutes everyone that was in on it was in trouble as the school tried to find out who had bought some of these bullets. The school wanted to deal with the matter itself rather than involve the police. And they didn't want the press getting hold of the story for reputational reasons.

Mr Lewis went absolutely mad. He was a known disciplinarian and I could hear him in full force as he literally threw people up against his office wall. Gal got the death poke; a firm poke Mr Lewis was well-known for. He really went to town on Dale and Cotton. I went in last but all he said to me was, "Martin, can you run to Crookhorn, the school next door and collect these books please?" When I got back he simply said, "That is your punishment." I was gobsmacked. Maybe in a twisted turn of fate, this beast of a Year Head saw something in me and was looking out for me.

How on earth this all happened to me, I have no idea. Nor do I know how parents of Jane and Peter dealt with it but none of us got expelled. Jane and Peter had been the only people that had come to Oaklands with me from my middle school. So I grew fairly close to them for that reason while we were in the First Year. Peter especially had been hugely supportive when he knew I was being bullied badly in the First Year. Well we all lived to tell the tale. To my recollection there was not even a suspension handed out and fortunately none of us got shot or blown to bits so that was a bonus. I guess it's the sort of morbid curiosity that children have that led Jane and Peter to pinch them and us to buy them and take them to bits.

Yet I was suspended for buying that bloody tennis racket of all things; it made no sense. But that was the one and only time I ever got suspended. We used the unexpected time off as an extension to the weekend and really enjoyed it. Except for the threat of expulsion, hanging over us, of course. We went to the cinema one day in Cosham and Dale was told he would have to pay adult as he was too old to go in as a child. The problem was he was so tall and went nuts, screaming, "I know how fucking old I am you knob." As things escalated, we ended up having to make a run for it. Don't get me wrong, I was generally a good kid in relative terms and hated being in trouble of any kind. But unsurprisingly the suspension caused problems at home.

Mr Lewis knew I was in love with Mandy yet he gave me the option to be with her. And to this day I can only assume he knew, that at this tender age, all your hormones are running wild and your first love is always so special. I used to melt when I looked at her and some twenty years later, I can still vividly remember the feeling of running my hands through her wonderful long, blonde hair. We used to write each other love letters almost on a daily basis and I have kept them all; they are one of my childhood treasures and I still have them tucked away to this day.

Unfortunately, things started to deteriorate with Mandy after about seven or eight months. She had come over to my house and we had been playing around in the bedroom. We never had sex but we were experimenting like all teens do and we both longed to be each other's first love. I remember holding her in my arms and gently touching her soft skin and tugging on her bra straps while she whispered sweet nothings in my ears; it was a lovely afternoon.

Unfortunately, Mandy wrote about it in her diary and her parents found it. She was grounded for six months. This was not the end of us because we still had our time together at school but one night my lodger, Jo, drove me and a few mates to Mandy's house in Clanfield, after we had all been drinking. What should have been a lover's serenade turned into a bit of a disaster. Cotton was sick on the pavement and Fizz kicked her neighbour's front garden wall over. I knew it was the end. Shortly after we split up, and over the coming months, I longed for her and watched as she started going out with older guys who all had cars. It was like someone reaching into your chest and ripping your heart out. I cried myself to sleep night after night and to this day certain songs still remind me of Mandy but hey, I guess we all had a first love, right?

Chapter Seven
A Right Mess

Two days before the end of school Fizz and I played truant. While we were at the local Spar shop, buying cigarettes, we bumped into someone from the Reservation who we vaguely knew. Everybody called him, Ozzie. He always had a yellow Sony ghetto blaster with him and you could generally tell where he was by listening out for the distant sounds of either Run DMC or Derek B. Ozzie had a couple of girls with him. We didn't know them but they were also playing truant. They were wearing short pleated school skirts, very long socks and their ties were tied the wrong way around, just like the girls in the movie St Trinian's. He explained that his parents were at work and he had just bought some cans of lighter gas, that he was planning to sniff back at his with the Squirters as he called the girls. "Yeah, guys come round, beats 'trundling' around all days," he said.

So we went to his house and all sat around messing in his lounge; for a house on the Reservation it was a nice place. You could tell that both his parents worked because it was nicely furnished with all mod cons and was pristinely clean with a lot of food in the cupboards. We sat in the lounge watching TV while Ozzie and the two girls were sniffing one can of gas after the other. Fizz and I weren't really into sniffing aerosols so we declined and watched as they all started acting crazier and crazier. After a short while Ozzie started getting flirty with one of the girls on the floor. We shouted at him to go upstairs and he dragged her upstairs to a bedroom. We could hear screaming and groaning with the headboard banging on the wall.

We had a spliff and then got the munchies so decided to raid the kitchen. Fizz was tearing everything out of the kitchen cupboards and throwing it all over the floor. He was like a wild beast grabbing food, sweets or any goodies he could get his hands on. We often went for long periods of time living on bare essentials so you never passed up the opportunity to eat. And Fizz could eat quicker than most dogs! He was going, "Yum, yoghurt." He would have a spoonful then throw it down onto the pile of discarded goods in the middle of the kitchen floor. We did the same with all the breakfast cereals, chocolate bars. Fizz finished it off by pouring milk all over me, followed by fizzy drinks and undiluted squash. I retaliated by pouring honey all over him, then coating him in Rice Crispies and finished it off by throwing flour all over him.

The kitchen looked wrecked and I mean really wrecked. We started smashing all the eggs on the ceiling and all the crockery and cups on the floor, with the help of the remaining girl, who was as stoned as we were. Despite all the noise Ozzie just carried on with the other girl upstairs. And then I found the drinks cupboard. It was packed full of vodka, Bacardi, whisky, port and beer. We all swilled a few mouthfuls. I got hold of the food blender and poured in a load from each bottle, threw in some strawberry yoghurts and blended it together to make some sort of punch. Fizz took the top off to do an inspection.

A Right Mess

Unfortunately, it was still spinning so this red, gooey mess was now splattered over every work surface as well as the ceiling. We also had it all over our school uniforms so looked a real mess; reminiscent of something in the Blue Peter kitchen. We couldn't stop laughing.

When the blender came to a complete standstill, we looked at the remains inside the blender. It was a red, curdled liquid that looked like it had been made in a lab. Unbelievably, we started drinking it. Ozzie came down the stairs with the girl and just started laughing at his trashed house. "Fuck it, give us a drink man." Then he got straight back on the gas with the girls. It was absolutely unbelievable. How could the guy not care that we had trashed half his house and drunk all his parents' booze?

To round it all off, he threw the remainder of the red juice in the blender all over me and Fizz while we were in the lounge. It went all over their beige carpet like a blood stain soaking in. Then Ozzie said, "Oh, man she kinda presses under your dick and when you cum it literally hits the ceiling. That was fucking ace that." And with that the girl dragged him back up the stairs. "You boys feel free to bang her mate." Fizz and I just looked at each other, "No, you're alright." The girl actually looked quite disappointed but we were having none of it.

Fizz went into the garden because Ozzie had said that was where all the frozen food was. Unable to get into the locked shed, he threw a tin through the window and climbed inside. There was a huge chest freezer packed full of goodies: pizzas, desserts, chicken wings, waffles and so on. We started throwing the entire contents onto the grass. We picked through and took what we wanted and then a frozen sausage food fight ensued in our now heavily drunken state. Then we decided to throw frozen food at the upstairs window where Ozzie was having round two with that girl.

The first few sausages bounced off the glass and the burgers just flew into the gardens either side. I picked up a frozen chicken and said "this will do it." In a really drunken state I threw it at the window. There was a loud bang and then the sound of shattered glass as the chicken hit its target. Then we heard Ozzie laughing with the girl. He stuck his head and naked torso out the broken window and said: "Fuck it man, it's cool. I was planning to run away for a few days as my parents are fuckers." The next thing we knew was a load of piss was being thrown on us from the upstairs broken window. Ozzie and the girl found it immensely funny. Next was a bucket of water as we hurled frozen food at the window.

We went inside and it turned into a full-on water fight. Anything that could hold water was being used to throw water over each other. And glasses full of water were being smashed against the walls. Everyone just laughed and carried on until we were all exhausted or sick from the drink.

By the time the antics were over the house was so wet that the wallpaper was peeling off the walls and there was water dripping from the upstairs through the light fittings. It was so bad that when you turned the lights off, they still buzzed and stayed on but only dimly. I will never forget that day as long as I live. The complete and willing destruction of an entire house, just for a bit of fun. I could not believe that Ozzie didn't care one bit. In fact, he encouraged us and even joined in. That kid must have really hated his parents.

Ozzie started sniffing lighter gas again and then stamped on the cans. He just left them there, in the lounge, along with all the other carnage and drug taking paraphernalia. His parents would see exactly what had been going on. Ozzie didn't make any attempt to hide the evidence of gas sniffing. Then he said, "Shit, time to go, my Dad will be home soon." He then picked up his damp ghetto blaster and put his jacket on before we all left with the girls. I can only imagine the looks on his parents' faces when they got in. Every part of the house was trashed. The smashed window, peeling wallpaper, frozen food, thrown all around the garden and the kitchen. Well, the kitchen was something else.

We merrily walked off and me and Fizz made our way home. When I got back my Mum took one look at me. "Oh my God, look at the state of you. What the hell has happened?" I simply replied, "It was the second to last day at school Mum, so I had a bit of fun outside the school gates." She briefly lost her temper but suspected nothing. I never did see Ozzie again. I often wonder how long it was until he could go home, after the antics that went on here.

Another odd character on the Reservation was my next door neighbour's son, who was about two or three years older than me. He was nicknamed Gary Ryan after Michael Ryan, the killer who committed a gun massacre in Hungerford in 1987. This was he was absolutely obsessed with anything military: guns, knives, uniform, boots, you name it. If it was military, he wanted it. The same went for every war film he could find. He watched those 80s Vietnam films, like Full Metal Jacket and Platoon over and over again until the tapes wore out.

The Reservation

During the recession the grass on the communal areas outside our houses used to grow to knee length. I would often see Gary crawling around in it with a knife strapped to his leg while wearing a green, military style T-shirt and camouflage trousers. He had an aluminium, military water bottle strapped to his belt and was wearing army boots. Often he would have some khaki material wrapped around his head like Rambo or The Goonies, depending on how you looked at it.

Gary loved the long grass. He used to claim he was going to join the Army when he was older. Often he would knock on my door to ask if I wanted to join in with his mini-military exercises. Sometimes I did, sometimes I didn't; it really depended how busy I was at the time. But I remember going out one day and as I got on my BMX I heard him screaming. He was in the long grass and had jumped to his feet and started crying and screaming like a baby. "Mum help me," he wailed. I looked at him and asked if he was okay. He looked at me and then started to cry again. Turned out that mini Rambo had only gone and crawled right through a big load of dog shit while he was practising his military manoeuvres in the long grass, and had started screaming for his Mum because he was smothered in it. I remember thinking: "Yep," proper military material you are: all VHS guts and glory.

A few months later he got an air rifle with a telescopic sight. It was cool enough but he kept shooting everything with it. You'd speak to him and he would make out he was some kind of National Guard or something. Birds in the garden were the first things he targeted. Then he decided to start shooting school kids on the way home. Our house was on the end and at the side of it we had a brick wall with a gate. Gary had already finished school and didn't work. So one day he let himself into my garden and set himself up in a firing position with his telescopic air rifle, aiming towards the woods. Then he went on something of a shooting rampage.

I got shot in the leg on the way home. I think he was aiming for my head. And Jane, who was about fifty paces behind, also got shot. I heard her squeal and turned round to see her rubbing herself. Then someone else got it. As I reached my house, I could see him laying down by the side of the wall laughing. I said, "Thanks for that," and pointed to my leg, "Now piss off."

Later that night I was washing up and could see a couple of policemen removing bin bags of stuff from his house. By the look of it they took everything; his guns, clothes and videos. I never saw him with any military gear ever again. And he never crawled around in the shit, in the long grass, again either.

The Reservation

Chapter Eight
Killing Time

When I look back on it, the children on the Reservation often got up to some odd things to pass the time. Aside from the normal petty crime that went on, the next most popular pastime was to set fire to things, along with vandalism, before anyone was old enough to drink or take drugs. The kids were particularly happy when these pastimes were combined. On some land near the shops at the bottom of Mill Road there was a social club called Wheelers. I never went there but heard it was pretty crap. That being said, it probably contained things that the local kids wanted like sweets and other items a social club would have.

Wheelers was a prefabricated concrete structure with a pitched roof. It had metal, shuttered windows - a must as it had previously been targeted by locals who smashed them. It also had a reinforced door. One day I passed it on my bike on the way to Jeff's and the kids were lighting a fire outside. I stopped to watch but they never managed to do anything to the actual structure. All they did was leave a large black stain on the wall.

A few days later BT was installing some new phone lines a hostel that had just been built next door to Wheelers. Over the weekend they left some of the poles on the floor. Inevitably it was only a matter of time until a gang of small kids, no older than about eleven or twelve, managed to lift one up. There must have been about thirty kids carrying this pole. It was like every kid in a two-mile radius had come to lend a hand. I was on my BMX and was just heading off to clean cars with Jeff. But because it was at the end of his road we decided to watch. Well, what can I say other than Braveheart would have been proud of this lot. It was a co-ordinated effort and now the BT pole was an effective battering ram. So they started battering the club's reinforced metal door. Over and over again they swung at the door. It made a really loud metal thud almost like a massive gong as they struck it again and again.

The door showed no signs of giving in so after about five or ten minutes one of the little kids told them to bring the pole around to the side of the building. They struggled under the weight and the uneven surface but the sheer weight of numbers managed to get it moved. Jeff and I then watched them pick it up and strike the concrete wall where there had been that fire a few days earlier. Almost immediately the battering ram started to pierce the wall. It seemed they had found the building's Achilles Heel and it was about to submit.

The kids stopped to have a peek through the small hole and then continued with the medieval assault. In less than ten minutes they had punched a hole big enough to get in. And ten minutes later the place had been robbed of all its goodies. And ten minutes after that it was on fire. I wish I could say that ten minutes after that a fire engine arrived. But I'm afraid not. Jeff and I just sat on our bikes watching the club burn while the kids ran around eating sweets and playing ping pong on the road.

Killing Time

That marked the bitter end of Wheelers Social Club. The kids who had masterminded the assault were right little local shits. They were very young and completely out of control. Their parents either chose to do nothing or turned a blind eye. But who knows? Perhaps they themselves were just victims of the Reservation or their own family circumstances.

You see the problem is that kids learn quickly. Word got round that this kind of medieval battering could smash walls. So the next thing you know, the doors at the back of the local shops were also smashed in with phone poles and emptied of cigarettes, drink and sweets.

Another property that was completely destroyed by children from the Reservation was a large and impressive house called Roach House on Purbrook Heath. It was not quite a mansion or stately home but, with its impressive brick pillars and a long drive that meandered down to it, it was close enough. Roach House itself was a lovely looking Victorian property on a substantial plot. We always thought it was funny that it shared its name with a spliff roach. So everyone would say let's go for a spliff at Roach House and more often than not we did.

I don't know who originally discovered that the house was empty and broke in but everything of value was long gone. By the time we started going there the windows were already smashed and you could see the thin bits of wood in the plaster that had been the walls in Victorian times. I remember the ceilings were rather high and there was a loft hatch. But what I found really strange was a set of footprints that ran straight up the wall and then underneath the ceiling. It was like some kid had been wearing anti-gravity boots or something. To this day I always wondered how they did it.

One day we arrived on our mopeds - BMXs were now a thing of the past - and after having a few spliffs thought it would be great fun to ride our bikes around the house. Some of the floors upstairs had holes in where people had lit fires but it never put us off. One by one we drove our bikes in there and started riding around the house, room by room. It was great fun. But then Swain got to the bottom of the staircase and just grinned in a way that you knew he was going to do something. Then without warning he drove his bike up the stairs.

It really struggled to get up there and you could see him wrestling with his feet to keep it going upwards. Once at the top he vanished but you could hear him screaming in delight as he went from room to room. I followed suit on my Trials bike. To be fair the bike handled it really well and sprung up the stairs but then the rest tried to follow. The mopeds with small wheels failed miserably on the stairs and ended up falling backwards until they gave up. After scrambling around upstairs for about twenty minutes, I put my bike on its stand under the loft hatch. I got one of the guys to hold it while I stood on the seat and pulled myself into the loft.

Like the rest of the house there was nothing up there except a few bits of rags and some old newspapers. Nevertheless I started to explore this large void. But then, after about twenty paces, the roof gave way and I was suddenly hanging from the loft with a long drop beneath me. My legs were frantically moving underneath me while I was desperately trying to pull myself up, back inside the loft. Everyone thought it was hilarious, well everyone except me who was fighting for my own non-broken limbed existence. I was screaming for help but just heard shouts of "fall you wanker" and "see if you can jump up there and grab his legs." Normally I would have joined in with the banter if it hadn't been me hanging out of the hole in the ceiling. And it was one hell of a long drop.

Somehow, and I have no idea how, I managed to find enough strength to pull myself up and edge gingerly back to safety. My legs had been cut to ribbons because I had fallen through some thin, jagged slats as the rotten wood gave way. I climbed down through the loft hatch and showed the guys all my cuts and bruises which they found immensely funny. I started my bike and began the nerve-racking descent down the staircase.

It had been far easier going up than going down. I couldn't control the bike and flew down to the bottom of the stairs. The bike jumped across the hallway and stopped when it hit the wall, with me still hanging on for dear life. There was one blessing; the whiplash took my mind off the cuts on my legs for a bit. I looked a right mess, bleeding and torn to bits. We all left in convoy after having a spliff for the road.

Another night we found ourselves at Roach House having a smoke and a beer on our motorbikes. I call them motorbikes in the loosest of terms because, with only 50cc engines, they were technically mopeds. However, I and a few others had given their bikes a little extra power. My bike was a trials bike, Swain's was an Easy Rider and the rest of the guys just had mopeds like Honda Visions or Honda Melodys.

Near Roach House was a pristine grass bowling green. As we

were all laughing and joking around, someone suggested we should go over and see if we could get onto the green. We rode our bikes up the road and sure enough the gate was open. Within minutes five or six of us were on this pristine grass doing doughnuts. My bike had off-road tyres and was ripping the turf clean off in long strips. I went round and round, laughing at the top of my voice. Being stoned really gave us all the giggles. This was a shocking act of vandalism. We all knew it was wrong but found it too funny to stop. Round and round we went, doing doughnuts until we were so dizzy we had to stop. And then, as if nothing had happened, we all went out the gate, across the grass and rode off in a long convoy.

I have often spent time thinking about the look on those poor people's faces when they saw what we had done the next morning. The green was always beautifully manicured and in less than five minutes us degenerates had completely ruined it, for a few cheap laughs, while we were high one night. The Heath was always such a popular place for mischief as it was the first really nice open space that was off the Reservation. And you could get to it by foot in about twenty minutes.

Not long after someone burnt Roach House to the ground and I have to say I really missed going to it for a spliff. I'm not sure how bad the fire was but a few people told me it had gone to the great house builder in the sky. Before you knew it they installed some big gates and demolished the remains. Then they built luxury new houses where Roach House once stood. We used to love the Heath. You could watch a leisurely game of cricket at the weekend or, as we got older, simply sit in the car in the car park. It was a

Sporting a little red stunner of a beat up old pedal car, I used to love this thing. I completely blame this little red car for what turned into a love affair I had with red Ferraris later in life.

I am not sure when this picture was taken, looking at it I guess I was about four or five years old at the time, but I do remember the jacket as I remember it kept me really warm.

A folk group performing in Greywell precinct, Leigh Park, as part of the adult education campaign did not seem to be appreciated by gun-totin' Martin Montague (four),

My first ever time in the press, I was blasting my cap gun at some local Folk Singers in Leigh Park. I still hate folk music with a passion, The Greywell precinct used to be a local bustling shopping centre for the estate. Today it is a deserted victim of out of town shopping and widespread car ownership.

Here I was with my first ever friends in Leigh Park, our house to back onto woodland where we used to play for hours on end day after day. We always loved the adventure of crawling around in the dirt and getting filthy to the annoyance of our parents.

I guess I must have been about seven or eight years old here, I was always a fairly "happy go lucky" child with a big cheesy grin.

Sporting one of my brother's crash helmets to go and play in the woods in. I guess I would have been about eight or nine years old when this picture was taken. I always looked up to my older brothers and wanted to follow in their footsteps.

Sporting my "grow into it bike" I re-member all too often crashing on this old second hand bike when I got it, as it was far too large for me to be able to touch the floor initially. I loved it until the day it got stolen by some larger kids while I was at the local park.

This was the day we moved into our new council house in Purbrook when I was about 10 years old. Our house was end of terrace and almost smack bang in the middle of the reservation.

Here I was on moving in day with my older brother Mark, he was always a legend in my eyes. You can see me lifting a demijohn bottle here that mum used to make her terrible home brew gut wrench in.

This picture was taken in Waggoners Wells near Greyshott, around 1982-3 on a day out with my Mums boyfriend at the time. I wonder if I ever did manage to catch lunch that day…

I was eleven or twelve years old in this picture, it was taken in the first year at Oaklands in Purbrook. Funny thing is this still feels like yesterday, note my distinctive mop head haircut that coined my nickname.

Here is a wonderful blunt that I rolled for a friend. This picture was taken with Kath in about 1999 when we had friends over for a BBQ. Whilst I rolled it and we had our picture taken with it we had both stopped smoking puff about five or so years before.

This picture was taken in about 1994 in our first house we owned in Portsmouth, we had lovingly papered it and hung new doors and made it out home. Our sofa had been bought from a chap that cleared our repositions through work at the time when we were both estate agents.

This was day when Kath made me the proudest man on earth in 1998. The wedding was great although the weather was terrible.

Here I am outside the church on our wedding day, despite all the rain it was probably the happiest day of my entire life.

Here I was standing proudly outside the car lot sporting my lovely overalls with our all-important customer satisfaction guarantee.

This is the mansion house that used to be called Sterns in Worthing, you can see the tea room on the very far right of the picture. The underground level was literally deep beneath the lawn area at the front of the picture.

Here is the flyer for the free rave festival Torpedo Town that I lost my raving virginity at. It was an absolutely awesome night and the kids of today will never know quite what the missed out on.

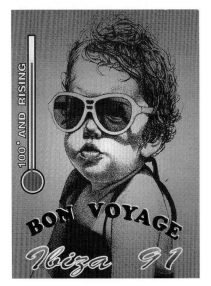

Here is the flyer from the very first time we ever went to the House on the Hill. It is now proudly framed among my other most precious possessions in my Man Cave.

As you can see some great DJs cut their names here and the giant party's and legendary nights out will stay with me forever. I can still remember being in the basement that night like it was literally yesterday.

Here you can see the seemingly never-ending stairway into the underground level of this super club. This picture evokes so many happy memories of passing happy people going up and down this long stairway. *Picture by Jonathan King.*

Just to give you an idea of how colourful and trippy the place was this is a picture of the mirrors in the underground that were coloured in trippy colours and shapes.

This is the stage where so many of todays leading acts played including The Prodigy and Moby. *Picture by Jonathan King.*

A great line up that night in this Victorian fort including a good friend of mine Bazz who went on to have a top ten release with a remix he did.

This flyer today lives proudly in my man cave, it was a great night out but was bitterly cold in the early hours of the morning.

This picture was taken at a Christmas party we went to in 1999. I always used to enjoy getting dressed up for a good night out.

really great place.

When the chips were down or turf wars with other Reservation residents came to a head, people would often come together to fight for a common cause. I remember that the estate in Wecock Farm had a crew called Wecock Wrecking Crew. They had been coming down in convoys of cars and stopping at the local park and shouting abuse. You know the way this goes: one gobshite from each side starts, but from a distance, until it's agreed that there will be a massive fight between the two sides at an arranged time.

Now let me tell you, if you haven't already figured it out, I am not the fighting type. Only if I can't really help it or am in a corner and have no option. But I did engage in the conversation about the forthcoming big battle in the park that was going to take place on Sunday afternoon. It was right up Dale's alley as he used to love a bit of a scrap and was kind of partial to a spot of football hooliganism.

Dale talked a good fight but was not a good fighter and he might have been tall but he was a lousy fighter. Once I watched in total disbelief as Dale got into a fight with someone half his size and was fighting him off like a girl. The guy simply put his hands on Dale's shoulders, jumped up and head-butted him. Dale fell to the ground and that was it.

Cotton loved a good scrap though and was a natural fighter. I watched him have a fight with a local kid called Reidy who kept saying he was going to beat Cotton up. Cotton was hardly bothered and just said: "Sure yeah, bring it on." Well I watched this fight with a morbid curiosity, along with another thirty or forty kids. Cotton lured Reidy onto a concrete car park rather than fight on the grass. As punches were flying, Cotton wrestled this kid to the ground and then grabbed his head and started banging it on the concrete like a melon.

I could barely watch as I thought Cotton was going to kill the kid. He grabbed Reidy by the throat and half strangled him, only stopping when Reidy agreed Cotton had won the fight and that he wouldn't bother him again. It was probably one of the best scraps I have ever seen. Cotton definitely under-estimated himself as a fighter. His ability to fight was far in excess of what he gave himself credit for in terms of the local pecking order.

Some other kids on the Reservation were handy too, especially those a few years older than us. It was these kids who were going to take the brunt of the Wecock Wrecking Crew. These guys had a reputation for being animals so we knew the big fight was going to get messy. In the days running up to the big fight it was the only thing anyone talked about. People said they were going but it was mostly just idle words.

On the day of the fight about twenty or so cars came down the road and stopped next to the park. You had the main contingent of people on the grass and they were gesturing for the guys to get out of the cars and fight. Behind them were a number of smaller kids who were preparing to throw things like bits of stone and brick. And behind that line you had the even smaller kids and cowards like me. I'm not ashamed to admit it but I didn't really fancy getting beaten up. And if the action got this far back, I had an escape route and was ready to run for it and take cover in someone's house. I thought that maybe if things were going our way I might advance forward a bit and throw a few stones. But I had a fairly decent view from where I was.

All of a sudden a few stones were thrown at the cars. In an instant the people jumped out and started running at the bigger Reservation kids who were our first line of defence. From my coward's position I could see people pulling at each other's clothes and hitting each other in the face. There were also a few people with tools like bits of wood and bats on either side. This fight looked pretty evenly matched for a few moments but as more and more of the Wecock Wrecking Crew got out of the cars it became apparent that although we were superior in numbers we were losing ground rapidly.

I could see our lads getting kicked on the floor and struggling to their feet and then getting another kicking. The second row of kids on the edge of the park started to fall back into the woods where we were. At this point I ran even further back to the very end of the small copse. More stones were thrown and there was screaming and shouting but it was obvious we had all had our asses kicked. Well, at least I could say I was there, albeit in a cowardly position behind the smallest kids at the back. Like I said, I am no fighter. I clearly knew my role was that of a gazelle on this game reserve. And no doubt about it, I was not going to change any time soon.

Over the coming weeks I heard that cars packed with Reservation people had gone to Wecock for pay back. But I'm not entirely sure that was true. It was more likely to be just another one of those urban myths.

The Reservation

Chapter Nine
What Highway Code?

This is a year I will always remember fondly, perhaps more than any other year. I had never felt closer to a circle of friends in my entire life. We were all young, free and single, without a care in the world. It was the year when we all became men and our very own Band of Brothers would have a fantastic and adventurous time, before life got too serious.

I vividly remember 7th of May 1990. It was raining really hard. That noisy, stinging kind of rain, when everyone runs for shelter. And it was the day of my driving test. To appreciate the importance of my test date, you firstly need to understand that it had been my seventeenth birthday on the 4th, just three days before the test. I had put in for an emergency cancellation when I was sixteen, asking for a test date just after my birthday. The plan was to pass my test by the summer so me and the lads could spend the holidays out and about. The only problem was that I hadn't had a single driving lesson in the three days since my birthday. Nor did I own a car or have any kind of insurance.

Never being one to give up, despite the odds, I asked my Mum if I could borrow her bright yellow T registration Fiesta. I told her that Dale had passed his test and was insured, so she agreed to lend me her car. For the three days before my test we just cruised around all over the place, without L plates while listening to rave tapes and getting stoned in Purbrook Heath. I could kind of drive anyway as I had learnt with some of the other guys who used to take us joyriding. But I had absolutely no concept of traffic lights, the Highway Code, roundabouts or anything like that. And most of my actual road experience had been driving when I was sixteen. I used to drive around my Mum's automatic Renault 18 after she went to bed, which she bought the year before when she got some money by starting a small cleaning business. But to be fair, within those three days, while getting stoned I did sit in the car with the guys and tried to learn the Highway Code.

My test was at 2.20pm and my brother Mark had said he would take me to the Test Centre, but only after I helped him put up a satellite dish in Leigh Park. As I helped him fit the dish, I thought I might as well 'skin up' and have a bit of spliff to calm my nerves while he was up on the roof. I slid out of sight and enjoyed the thick smoke filling my lungs along with the warm, carefree feeling that slipped over my body. I can remember thinking to myself, I'm soaking wet from the rain, about to take my driving test, without ever having a proper driving lesson. I have no car insurance, little knowledge of the Highway Code and was only legally old enough to learn to drive barely three days ago... Oh, and now I'm stoned. I started to giggle but then I looked at my watch: We were going to be late.

I hurried Mark up as best I could but sure enough, we arrived at the Test Centre in Eastney nearly five minutes late. As I ran into the waiting room the examiner was calling my name. There was no time to even anticipate what was going to be in the test. First he checked my vision, then he checked my details and we got into the car. Fortunately, in the early 90s they never checked to see if you were insured so that was a bonus.

I thought I would drive slowly and steer like a proper 'pleb' without crossing my hands. I was pretty chilled out and focused as I was still stoned and after about five to ten minutes the guy began to chat. Firstly, about the weather and then he started talking about his messy divorce. I reversed faultlessly around a corner and did a superb three-point- turn and then we headed back to the Driving Centre. He asked me some Highway Code questions.

Fortunately, the first couple were common sense but then he showed me a circle with an arrow pointing to the left. Having hardly looked at the Highway Code I had no idea, so shrugged my shoulders and started to laugh, as this whole test thing was like one big joke. But then he said, "Ok Martin, let's put it another way. If you came across this sign with the arrow pointing left, would you drive on the left or right hand side of it?" After a split second I said: "Left." He smiled and said, "Mr Montague, I am pleased to inform you that you are a very safe and competent driver and that you have passed your driving test."

Every single hair on my body stood on end as disbelief raced through my veins. I looked at him again expecting to hear he was only joking. I mean seriously, what were the chances of a pass in these circumstances? No lessons, no insurance, three days experience with my friends, who couldn't drive properly, along with a few 'driving lessons' from the local joyriders. Yet I had actually done it. I had passed my driving test first time. None of my friends believed me until I proudly showed them my pass certificate.

My Mum still had her old automatic Renault 18 and was so pleased I'd passed my test that she gave it to me. My brother Mark fixed it all up for me. Summer had begun.

I still didn't have any insurance but we went everywhere in this car. It had a massive sun roof that rolled back and a decent enough cassette player. To this day I still have the old rave tape that we played day after day, hour after hour. We would park under a big oak tree in Purbrook Heath and get stoned; open the doors and dance the night away.

Having a car opened up so many doors. Racton Ruins was a large tower near Emsworth and was one of our favourite spots. We used to drive up the hill to the 'Devil Worshiping Centre' of Hampshire for a laugh. It was already a creepy place with pentagrams and weird markings inside the derelict tower. But one night it was really misty which made the place a lot scarier.

We couldn't believe it when we saw a long line of 'Devil Worshipers' walking through the mist, about twenty feet away from the car. They were all wearing long, dark cloaks like monks. Until then we all assumed these stories of devil worshippers was an urban myth. We took one look and everyone started screaming. I immediately jumped in the car and locked Fizz out. We all thought it was really funny but he started screaming like a girl. Then, as I reversed down the hill, Fizz lay flat on the bonnet and clung on for dear life. When I stopped and let him in, he was not amused.

After about a month of trying to look after my pride and joy, the car was showing the scars of pot smoking. The interior was littered with burn holes. The previously sumptuous, grey velour was now punctuated with tiny little holes, all caused by hot rocks falling onto it.

Women were always on the agenda for us. None of us had one but we all wanted one. Dale had stolen some of his Dad's porn magazines and we would often stop and read them while enjoying a spliff. Fizz also made a sign for the back window that said, 'Whores wanted, apply within'. It never actually worked but was funny nonetheless. While driving home one night with Fizz, we noticed two attractive girls walking down the road. I recognised one of them as Kath and the other one was her friend Tina. I had been out with Kath when I was about thirteen but she had dumped me for an older local guy who everyone thought was an idiot. We pulled over and gave them a lift home. Tina remarked, "Fucking nice stereo," and then asked, "You got any gear? We wanna get stoned." Fizz passed a spliff around. Before we dropped them off, we stopped the car and had a real laugh and a joke.

I was really attracted to both of them and over the coming weeks they were regular passengers as we drove around. One night we were up on Portsdown Hill and started play-fighting with the girls; it ended up getting a bit frisky. A few days later I asked Tina out but she refused; I have to say that I still have no idea why. She did have a bit of a 'je ne sais quoi' quality about her so I was quite disappointed at the knock back. But then, over the next few weeks, I became more and more attracted to Kath. We got on like a house on fire. When I asked her out a few weeks later, I was really pleased when she said yes.

Kath had a really nice glow about her. I remember that at the time she had bleached, blonde hair and was really into Madonna.

The Reservation

When the girls used to knock on my door my Mum used to come and get me and say, "Dracula's daughter's at the door." You know how it is, no girl is ever good enough for a Mother's son.

My Mum has always been hugely artistic and loved the garden. She would spend every spare moment either moulding objects out of Plaster of Paris and painting them, or doing still-life landscapes in pastels. Her garden was like a little piece of paradise. One day someone randomly knocked on the door and asked if she wanted to buy a set of large, concrete lions for the garden. They were not expensive and she jumped at the chance. These lions stood proudly at around three feet tall and it took two chaps to carry each of them in from the van to the back garden. There they had pride of place amongst a few gnomes that she had painted and her well-tended flowers.

The lions stood proudly on guard for several years until one of them was randomly acquired from the back garden. Even in Reservation terms this was a fairly odd theft. Why would someone climb over a six-foot wall to steal one three-foot concrete lion? I couldn't see our lion being in the back of the Yugo Boys' car up on the top of the hill, being traded for drugs. The size and weight alone would make it practically impossible!

About three months later Mum was in a fluster. "Martin I have found our lion," she said. I looked at her and asked, "Where?" She said she would show me when it was dark. That night Mum took me for a walk and we gingerly peered over someone's wall. And there, in all its glory, was our lion in the back of someone else's back garden.

The place was like a fortress. It had broken glass cemented

onto the top of the wall and a large padlock and chain around the gate. "Mum, there is no way on earth I can get that back. Look at the glass, look at the wall." But Mum went on and on about it, day after day, week after week along with my girlfriend Kath until I agreed to somehow try to steal it back for her.

So one dark night I took Kath with me and we set off to get the lion back. It was about 3am and no one was around. I had brought an old towel with me and started snapping all the bits of glass off, that were poking out of the top of the wall. I cleared a section about a metre wide - this was a trick we'd all learnt from Cotton. I folded the towel up several times and placed it on the cleared piece of wall. Hopefully, this would stop any remaining glass cutting me as I went over. I scaled the wall and jumped into the garden on the other side.

Slowly I made my way over to where the lion was standing. I could hardly lift it but somehow managed to tilt it and drag it quietly across the lawn until I was at the point where I had climbed over the wall. Then I whispered to Kath, who was still on the other side, to stand clear. After several attempts I managed to lift it up onto a log. After several failed attempts and nearly giving up, I managed, somehow, to get the lion up to my chest and then threw it over the top of the wall, onto the grass on the other side. I heard a dull thud as it landed and asked Kath if it was okay?

At that point the neighbour's dog stirred so I got back over as fast as I could and wrapped the folded towel around my neck. I didn't want to leave any evidence. We then carried this lion all the way home. Kath had the lighter end while I carried the base; it was backbreaking work. We got it to the front door, took it through the house and placed it in the back garden, in the exact spot it had been stolen from. We then quietly crept back into the house and went to bed.

The next morning, I woke up and looked out the window. To my horror I could see that the lion we had brought back was a clear six inches shorter than the original. Now you don't need to be Sherlock Holmes to realise that your successful evening raid to repatriate your stone lion, was now a criminal offence.

I showed my Mum and there was no doubt about it, this was not our stone lion. My Mum started laughing, "I was sure it was ours." We could have killed her but we did see the funny side. I had to drag that thing indoors and stick it in the coat cupboard. And there it stayed, for about five years, until one day the lion went back into our garden where it proudly sat, admittedly six inches lower than the other one. To my knowledge my Mum still has both lions, and whenever I bring this story up, she still finds it immensely funny.

When you have next to nothing and live on somewhere like the Reservation, the simplest things in life can be really important to you. A hot bath, a warm jumper, some decent toilet paper or even a tin of beans. Unless you have lived in abject poverty you will struggle to appreciate the small luxuries in life. If you scrimp and save for things, even if those things are second hand, it is something to be proud of. We had a top loading video recorder. Now I know that by now ninety-nine per cent of Britain had one, so what was so special about ours? All I can say is that we were probably in the last one per cent to have a video player so it was a big achievement in our little world.

What Highway Code?

The last thing I expected was to be burgled. My Mum was devastated. Some shits had broken in and acquired our video. I mean what kind of druggy, scumbags would do such a thing? The cheeky shits had even made themselves a bit of toast, after forcing their way in. We were now back in the one per cent of people without a video and the gaping big hole under the rented TV was an ominous reminder of what had been stolen. Aside from the loss of this treasured asset, it was the fact that your property had been violated.

I immediately suspected Cotton because he was always hungry and had form, but I knew deep down he would never do such a thing. Although he used to try to improve his lot, he always robbed from strangers. To be fair he did practise the thieves' code, and whoever took it would have to look you in the eye and I don't think Cotton would be able to do that. That left Neil and Chaps but realistically, it could have been any number of people from this hell hole.

Swain seemed genuinely concerned that my Mum was so upset about the burglary and the loss of the video and offered to sell us an old Betamax video for £20 that used to belong to Alison before she left his dad. Although Betamax videos were virtually obsolete, my Mum agreed to buy it and gave him a few quid a week until it was paid for. She seemed fairly happy although renting Betamax tapes was all but impossible. Swain showed he was a true friend to me by doing this and accepting a few quid from my Mum every week. Well, that's what I thought at the time. I later found out that it had been Swain and Gal who had burgled my house. Gal confessed about fifteen years later.

The Reservation

It turned out they had taken my video to the top of Portsdown Hill and swapped it for drugs with the Yugo Boys. It wasn't a pretty thing. These dealers had my video and I would never see it again.

A few years later Gal's posh house in Widley got burgled. His parents had always assumed he was an innocent child until the robbers broke in and turned the place upside down. They sprayed on the walls that he was a drug dealer. Initially it was assumed that Chaps had done it but the thieves also sprayed 'This is phase one' on the wall. Now without being Columbo, the word 'phase' in Reservation terms, was quite a tricky word to spell. Almost everyone would have spelt it 'Faze' and all the usual suspects could hardly read or write, so it looked like an inside job. I feel he got his just desserts after burgling my house with Swain so have no compassion for him. One thing was almost certain. His stuff probably ended up on the Hill, in the boot of that red Yugo but we will never truly know for sure.

This was also the year I got a glimpse of how the other half lives. Fizz had become friendly with a girl called Mollie who was in the year below us at school. I'm not sure if they were actually going out together or just good friends but she was a great girl for a number of reasons. Firstly, her Dad was some American high flyer at IBM who had moved over here with work. Secondly she was a great looker and had this really cute American accent and lastly she was loaded: proper loaded with extra loaded on top.

When we went to her house in Hayling, you left the road and drove down this long sandy track. Then you went down a gated drive and you were faced with this modern mansion style house, that sat impressively on its own sandy beach. It was huge; it looked like one of those houses you see on TV that are owned by drug dealers.

The house had a manicured lawn, lovely ornaments and a fountain in the front garden and two large doors that opened onto an impressive hallway with a marble floor. I'm pretty sure this was the nicest house I had ever seen, let alone been in. I stood for several minutes just looking around at the opulence that surrounded us. The kitchen was twice the size of our houses put together. And because we were always on the look-out for food, we noticed the American style double door fridge. We looked at each other and just said "Yum" before succumbing to temptation and opening it. Mollie said, "Help yourselves guys but there is not a lot in there at the moment; just don't make a mess."

When we opened these two doors a cool glow shone over what looked like a chilled delicatessen. There was a range of chilled meats, salad items, yogurts, milks, various drinks, beer. It was like we had died and gone to heaven.

About seven or eight sandwiches later, we went for a walk along her private beach and then sat outside by the pool. I sat there thinking this is the life. Imagine all the opportunities this girl would have. It didn't bear thinking about. It was a Beverly Hills 90210 lifestyle right here on the South Coast of England. We were just a couple of oiks from a place that everyone wanted to forget even existed. But for the next hour or so, as we had a drink and chatted by the pool, I took a mental imprint of what having money was like. And I can tell you I really liked it.

From this point onwards it was a dream that I knew I wanted to chase and could understand why it meant so much to so many people. But for now it was just a dream and a lovely dream. Well it was until Fizz threw me and the chair I was sitting in into the pool, where I sank to the bottom, still holding onto the arm rests. After I pulled my sodden self out we all ended up in the water along with the pool furniture. It was a fantastic day out, just to see how the other half lived.

Chapter Ten
Young Gangsters

The rave years were in full swing and everything seemed so beautiful. The drugs, the music, the women, the weather; it was all perfect. But I needed a job. I knew I was better than this place. At times it had touched me in a good way but at other times it had emotionally scarred me. Escape was going to be the problem. How do you get out of a place like the Reservation other than by crime or benefits with no GCSEs?

Personally I have always been hugely driven. The deprivation, crime and death that surrounded me was not the way of life I wanted. Day after day I promised myself that I would somehow escape the chains of this place. But when it's all you've ever known, escape seems impossible.

I had got my first taste of sales as a door-to-door canvasser for a company called Leisure Studios in Fareham. It was a kitchen, bedroom and bathroom design company. It was one of those jobs where you turned up for an interview because you were still at school and needed the money. But as you didn't have any qualifications you were limited on what you could actually do.

I went to the careers centre in Waterlooville and noticed a job for a trainee car salesman in Portsmouth. I enquired about it but the lady behind the desk said that over one hundred people had already applied and the ad was just about to be taken down as it was almost certainly filled. I begged for her to put my name forward so she called the garage, which was called Cheap Wheels, and got me an interview. I turned up smartly dressed and listened intently to what the owner Colin was saying. He was a really likeable fellow - funny and quick-witted. He also he looked a little like Colonel Gaddafi – although I never told him that!

As I sat there I realised this was my big chance to do something with my life, to break the bonds and get away from factory work. I asked him some questions and then I said, "If you give me this job, I will work for free to show you that I have what it takes. I just need an opportunity to prove myself." I still vividly remember what I said, word for word, even after all these years and what happened that day. And I still get emotional when I think about it.

Colin looked at me and then he said, "Martin over 100 people have applied for this job. You can see there are more people waiting outside to see me."

He then sat back on his chair, lit a cigar and said, "But you stand out like a shining star. I have heard enough. You start on Monday and you will get paid."

I had a really fun time working at the garage. Colin and I got on like a house on fire and boy, could I sell cars. Colin ended up like the father I never had and still remains one of the kindest people I have ever had the pleasure to know.

Working in the garage gave me a great sense of achievement. I was to be a trainee car salesman. It meant that one day I would be a real life salesman. I daydreamed about wearing a lovely pinstripe suit, a white shirt and silk, blue tie matched with some wonderful cufflinks. And I'd be working in a top car dealership. Well, that was my end game but the starting point was rather different.

The garage itself was an old, dome-shaped, open plan building, situated in one of Portsmouth hundreds of identikit small roads. At the end of the day we pulled these folding doors across that had a small entrance door in the middle with a letter box. And when we turned up in the morning, we'd open up and then move the cars around, so a couple were on the front half of the kerb. Behind the showroom was a muddy outdoor yard and behind that was our workshop and spray shop.

In terms of staff there was Colin the owner, who was a lovely guy, despite looking like the Libyan dictator. He would often be seen smoking a Hamlet cigar and was super confident on the phone or with people. Once you got to know Colin he was extremely likeable, hardworking and admirable in so many ways. But he also enjoyed a few beers and was known to get his own back on customers if they rubbed him up the wrong way.

His son Pete also worked at the garage. He had blonde flicked hair and looked like something off a World War II poster advertising the Master Race. Pete, whilst very good looking, seemed to be a bit simple and clumsy but hey, he was the boss's son and fun to work with. Pete would often skateboard into work and you could hear him and his friends' boards rattling as they skated over the square paving stones outside the showroom.

In the workshop out the back was a chap called Shane. He was such a gifted mechanic it was unreal. Shane could rebuild any gear box, weld several cars together like new and he could spray like a dream; Shane was a real all-rounder. He was very skinny and was always covered in oil. For months he used to just live and sleep in the workshop. We used to find him asleep on his dolly under a car or kneeling down on the floor, with his head in his arms facing one of the seats. Skills aside, Shane had this habit of leaving jobs unfinished and would often try to force his opinion on you.

There was also a mechanic called Eddie who drove a pumped up black Cortina. To be fair it was a kind of cool car that he had done a lot of work on. He'd managed to do all this work despite losing a few fingers in a previous job. Eddie was thick set with dark hair and not to be messed with; he could fly off the handle in less than a second. And then there was Ted who was Colin's father-in-law. He would help out generally and keep things tidy. Ted was retired and would often tell me funny stories. 'Life according to Ted' meant that Ted thought he was an expert on everything under the sun. But he was so likeable you couldn't help be fond of him.

I remember one day Ted asked me if I had a girlfriend. When I said yes he replied, "That's great, make sure you make love to her twice a day, every day, that's an order." When I asked why he explained, "Life is a question of using your best assets while you can. When you get to my age it's like sticking a marshmallow through a keyhole." This has always stuck in my mind as I found it so funny.

I recall thinking that he should work for the Government, doing some kind of job creation programme during the recession. Ted could make a full day's work out of sweeping one small area. He could often be found sweeping the puddles away in the yard while it was raining. He would sweep them, they'd fill up again and so on. We used to sit there and watch him hour after hour doing this never ending work.

Well, when I started work instead of a smart suit I was given a set of red overalls. It was Colin's idea. He thought customers would be more impressed by a mechanic showing them around a car. It seemed to work and I enjoyed my new job a lot. I would drive cars around, speak to customers and cleaned all the cars. I cleaned cars until my hands felt like they were about to fall off. I had to polish all the cars in the showroom every few days and dust them on the days in between. It was very hard work especially in the winter months. Although there was a roof on the showroom it could still be bitterly cold.

As time went on I would also help out in the workshop and the spray shop. I don't know how most other small garages operated but a few of the things that went on there were both funny and sad and will forever be engrained on my mind.

Colin meant well and really wanted to offer great customer service and satisfaction. Or at least he set out to do that. But all too often things went badly wrong. Firstly, I should point out that if you ever give a small garage or car sales place a hard time, bear in mind some of the things that went on at Cheap Wheels.

My first real insight into 'customer service' came when late one night I came across everyone in the workshop sharpening up screwdrivers on the grinder before they headed off for the pub. We played some pool at the Pelham Arms and afterwards Colin and the mechanics did some extra-curricular activity. They used to keep a book of 'bad customers' and would make a note in the diary to pay a 'visit' six months later so there was never any suspicion. These evening service calls would consist of either keying every panel of the car, puncturing tyres, or throwing paint stripper all over it. It really depended on just what a pain in the ass the customer had been. But inevitably, if you ended up in the Special Service book you would pay at some point. On this particular occasion I found out the next day that a blue Volvo had been keyed on every panel with these sharpened screwdrivers. The nice customers got nothing but great service but the horrible ones were destined for our Special Service.

I remember a few things that stuck out at the time as being either really funny or quite sad, depending on how you looked at it. One day we were weighing a 'breaker' in. It was an old Cortina and we'd cut the roof off with an air saw and stuck a left over pizza on the bonnet from the night before. We also sprayed the words 'Pimp Bus' down the sides and filled it with scrap. When cars were in for a service or repairs we always drove them for day to day things. If anyone ever asked why the mileage was different, we'd say it was simply a 'test drive'.

On this particular occasion Pete was using a customer's Alfa Romeo to tow me in the Cortina. We were going through the centre of North End and I was standing up in the 'scrapper' like a Roman driving a chariot. Everyone was stopping to look at our work of art. Pete stopped at a roundabout and only then did it dawn on me there were no brakes. I screamed as the Cortina crashed straight into the back of the customer's Alfa Romeo. Pete didn't seem to care and decided to 'wheel spin-off.' But as he did so the Cortina ripped the rear bumper straight off the Alfa. It turned out that Pete hadn't tied the tow rope properly.

I was now stuck half way across the roundabout. Pete reversed back up and I tied the rope on again while he threw the bumper in the back of the car. About an hour later the customer came in screaming that he had just seen his car towing a 'scrapper' and having its bumper ripped off. All this while his car was supposed to be in for a service. Oops!

Another customer was so irate with Colin on the phone that they both lost their temper. Colin decided to go to his house and give him a piece of his mind, face to face. He brought one of the mechanics and drove down to Hilsea. Colin started screaming and knocking on the windows and then shouted through the letter box. He could see they were in but were not coming to the door. Furious he picked up all the terracotta plant pots in the front garden and shouted, "I'm going to teach you a lesson, you ignorant bastard." Then he started smashing them on the concrete path, one by one. Next he ripped out all the plants in the front garden. Hearing all this commotion, one of the neighbours came out and to everyone's complete astonishment it was the customer who had complained. It turned out that Colin was at the wrong house. He beat a hasty retreat.

All too often we ended up in the pub, after work, and stayed until closing time. Sylvia, Colin's wife would often come looking for him and he would hide in the toilets or run out the back door. The landlord and staff always denied that he had been there. I remember one morning opening up the garage and a neighbour, who had bought a car from us and lived near the garage, telling me that his car had been stolen the night before from outside his house. He was clearly distressed and couldn't get to work and was waiting for the police. At that moment Colin turned up in the neighbour's car! He had been so pissed the night before that under a street light the car looked yellow, like the Cavalier he was driving and not the blue it actually was.

I have no idea how but in his drunken state he somehow managed to get into the car and got it started with the wrong set of keys. Apparently it was only after he sobered up the next morning and saw the neighbour's car outside his house, next to the Cavalier, that he slowly put two and two together. I watched as Colin gave him his car back and confidently explained the simple mix up. I was absolutely gobsmacked at how he could talk his way out of anything. Colin had such a silver tongue.

When the really difficult customers came in everyone used to hide. It was comical as the whole place turned from a garage into the Mary Celeste. Colin would hide on the flat roof or in the rafters of the workshop while I would run and hide under a car that was displayed in the showroom on a ramp. Everyone else would take their chances. Quite rightly these customers would come in day after day and expect their cars back, but more often than not they might have come in just for a bit of warranty work. Shane had started robbing bits from these cars and using them for other jobs, so before you knew it, these cars needed a lot more doing to them as they were being regularly stripped of parts. A vehicle could be at the garage for months instead of weeks.

I remember one poor customer coming in and Colin didn't hide in time. The customer watched as he climbed up into the rafters of the workshop. "Colin, I know you're there." He was rumbled so replied, "I'm mixing paint so can't come down.

Can you come back later?" This only aggravated things and the customer refused to budge. For the next hour or so they traded insults and then, unable to escape, Colin threw a container filled with piss down at the customer. I stood there laughing at the sheer vulgarity of it all as the pee soaked the customer. He made a swift retreat but threatened to call the police.

Another day Pete and I hid under a van in the yard as the same customer returned. Pete must have left his feet poking out a bit as he was swiftly dragged out from underneath the van; foot first. I could hear him lying about the customer's car and Colin's whereabouts. It got so bad for these poor people that the mechanics would pretend to be fixing their car by putting an engine lift over the open bonnet and scatter empty coffee cups nearby. After about eighteen months I think they reported the customer's car stolen and a friendly scrapyard 'lost it'.

Another time armed robbers brought in a car to sell. The police descended pretty swiftly and arrested them; the shotgun was still in the boot of the car! The garage really was an eye opener. The things that happened from day to day were sometimes surreal. Screw a set of number plates from that car onto this car and take that one for an MOT. Put glue in that person's petrol cap; 'no problem' and so on and so on.

I remember one day a 'special customer' coming in. They'd had glue put in their petrol cap. "Please help me, some hooligan has stuck glue in my petrol cap." Little did they know that it was this very garage who was the culprit. Now the poor guy was begging for help. "Mary has bible classes, please help me, please." I have to say this guy was normally a real pain and this was the first time I had ever seen him being nice. Colin smiled sweetly at him and then looked in the diary. "Oh, that's terrible, how does three weeks Friday sound? I'm sorry we are fully booked until then." The customer left and we laughed about it for weeks. This was a normal day in the garage.

Another customer rubbed Colin up the wrong way so he sprayed 'traffic film remover' in his eyes. The police were called to that one. Another day an irate customer came in and hit me in the face in sheer frustration over their car. I had explained that I was unable to help as Shane was dealing with it and they just flipped out.

The days were long, the work was hard and the winters were cold but I still enjoyed my work. I loved cars. I loved driving them, selling them, cleaning them, and working on them. One night a customer started kicking the front door and looking through the letter box. Colin had told him to collect his car at 5.30pm but then told me to close the doors at 5pm to avoid him as his car still wasn't ready. The customer was furious. He was screaming and peering through the letter box and kicking the large wooden doors.

Colin got so annoyed he came out of hiding to tell him to stop kicking the doors and go away. "Every time you kick my doors in, I'm going to kick your car." The guy went quiet for a moment and then started kicking the garage doors a few more times before peering through the letter box again. As soon as Colin knew he was looking, he took great joy in kicking his car a few times. This happened several times until the doors were dented and he said, "I told you not to do that," and the customer left. I can only imagine what must have been going through his mind.

Once the guys dunked me head first in a drum of used engine oil. Then I headed off to Kath's and knocked on the door and stood well back. Kath's Mum just looked at me as if to say, "What the hell is that?" It was really hard to get the oil out.

Practical jokes were all too common while working at the garage. Shane could be an asshole and would often come over to Pete and me and thrust a cup towards our chest and say "Tea." This went on for months until one day I said to him "One spit or two?" From that day on he never asked us again. To be fair we had been to the chemist and put laxatives in his tea. We also spat in it, put his cup in the toilet and did other monstrous things to it in order to make us feel better.

Shane insisted we had a drinks machine because he was wasting too much time brewing up. Colin got a Maxx Pax; you would fill it with cold water and the cups already had tea and coffee in them. When Shane was particularly hideous to us, we would throw dead rats in the water. Or another funny trick was to get a Stanley Blade and cut vertical slits down the side of the plastic cups. Then when he used to pick them up and squeeze them the hot tea or coffee would pour all over him. Of course neither of us knew anything about this? What, us? Surely not.

Shane decided he wanted a dog so he got one and called it Charlie. It was a vicious thing; I mean a really vicious thing. It was a lurcher crossed with something. I'm guessing the something was probably the nastiest something that someone could find. I love animals but this dog scared me. Pete took it for a walk one day to the chip shop and he came running back with it shouting "Hide!" Apparently Charlie had ripped out a Poodle's throat, killing it, so

The Reservation

Pete had run away. Another night Shane's girlfriend was visiting him at the garage. Charlie was very protective of Shane and he was asleep under a car when she turned up. Thinking she was an intruder Charlie attacked her and ripped her face to bits. I can't remember the exact number of stitches she had, but I think it was into the hundreds.

I remember once, while Colin was away on holiday, I decided to pass the time by having some 'gear yogurt.' Basically you mixed some puff with margarine, heated it over a lighter until it turned into a liquid and then stirred it into a yogurt and ate it. This seemed like a really good idea at the time as obviously I couldn't smoke a joint at work. But because I'd eaten it I was stoned on another level. I had gone way beyond my comfort level and ended up crawling around in the snow in the yard on all fours, doing snow angels. I couldn't speak coherently to customers and it took me hours to straighten up.

Chapter Eleven
The House on the Hill

How can you even start to explain the rave years of the early 90s to someone who never witnessed it first hand? It was so colourful, vibrant and energetic; a scene that words struggle to describe. It's hard to paint a picture of how brilliant it was. This period of my life was one of the most exciting times and will stain every memory until the day I die.

Firstly, you need to imagine the backdrop. It was the time of a tough recession and there were over three million unemployed. There had just been a massive resurgence in the drug culture that was similar, in a lot of ways, to the 60s. Pretty much everyone that you knew your age was smoking pot, at the bare minimum. And massive amounts of people were taking trips and speed on a regular basis. Because drugs heighten your senses, there's something about rave music that made you want to get up and dance. Every beat felt hypnotic, every song seemed to reach into your soul and stick in your head.

This music was the backdrop to everything we did. Every song was infectious and we listened to the same mix tapes, from our favourite DJs, again and again while smoking pot, whenever we could. We listened to the stories, told by those a little older than us, of raves that went on for days in fields or abandoned factories.

The Reservation

The love of the music made us aspire to go more and more. Several times we tried. Convoys of cars would head for Portsdown Hill, supposedly on their way to a rave, so we would often tag along. But we never managed to actually find one. You really needed to be in the know or know someone if you were to stand a real chance. Everyone said they'd been with a friend of a friend but more often than not they hadn't been either.

Stories circulated of a new rave wonder drug called Ecstasy along with tales of women dancing topless all night long. And the music seemed to be advancing in an underground way, week by week, luring us just like the sirens lured sailors to the rocks. Finding our first rave was more of a coming of age thing to us than losing our virginity, getting a job or learning to drive. It was all we ever talked about, day in day out. We would sit there rolling spliff after spliff talking about how we were going to find one or someone who could help us.

One night in July 1990 I ended up in a local pub called The Leopard. We could get served there, even though we were underage. We'd down Pernod and blacks and a Snakebite and black. I have no idea why but everything used to have blackcurrant with it but it didn't stop us getting wasted, despite tasting awful. I was with one of my friends called Jeff and we ended up getting legless with a local drug dealer called Nash. By closing time, it was one of those nights when we were too drunk to walk home. Fortunately, or unfortunately I had driven so we had a last shot each and stumbled outside to have a spliff before we virtually crawled into the car. Now drink or drug driving was so normal in those days on the Reservation that it hardly even raised an eyebrow. Being stoned was considered super safe believe it or not as there were no tests for it. You could be completely off your tits and clear a breath test with impunity despite being far less able to drive.

Nash asked for a lift home in exchange for some free gear. I agreed and everyone piled into the car. Then all of a sudden he goes, "Let's go raving. There is a big one on tonight and I know where it is." Jeff and I looked at each other; we were both blindingly drunk and said, "Hell yeah." So we headed for Petersfield. On the way we continued to get stoned and I had to stop the car to let Jeff out to be sick. We had rave music pumping out of the stereo. We were all in the mood for it.

We had just got past Petersfield when the road towards London was closed. Nash told us to park up as we needed to walk the rest of the way. We had no idea how far it was but I never imagined it would be a half marathon along the road. We parked down a side road and walked past the police roadblock, down the A3 towards London. We walked for about two hours along the eerily closed A3 until we were near Bramshott Chase. It was very surreal as you never really get to walk down the middle of a busy A-road like that; it was like something out of a post-apocalyptic movie.

All of a sudden Jeff said: "Listen." We all stood still. You could hear the dull rhythmic thud, thud, thud in the distance. It sounded like fireworks going off until we realised that must be the rave! As we drew closer we could see the clouds being lit up with a searchlight in the distance, it was like a lighthouse showing us the way. My legs turned to jelly and I could barely walk and was trembling with nervous anticipation. My hands were clammy and all my senses were heightened. This state was later called 'PRT' -

short for 'Pre-Rave Tension'.

As we got closer, we walked down a dirt path on the side of the road and spotted a police van parked next to it. Several policemen were standing there in full riot gear. As we walked past them I remember one of them saying, "Have a good night in there fellas." It struck me as a little odd, as it was more akin to a doorman at a club rather than a copper at a rave. We walked down this sandy dirt path that was surrounded by oak trees in a dark tunnel, and the music got louder and louder until we ended up walking into a valley. There were hundreds of cars, converted coaches, camper vans, old buses and old Post Office vans for as far as you could see. It was a truly awe inspiring sight. They were all parked randomly around the place with people sitting or dancing next to camp fires. Then, right in the middle of this valley there was a scaffold structure with lights beaming off it. Initially it looked like a UFO as all the drifting smoke was being filtered through the lights. Powering this light and sound monster was an old fire engine, and its searchlight was what we had seen lighting up the clouds on the way there.

As we walked the final quarter mile or so towards the rave, I shook with nervous anticipation and took long drawn out drags from the spliff we were smoking. As we walked past groups of new age travellers you could hear them shouting out, "Tongs, knives, a quid," or "Acid for two, pot for ten." We bought some gear and even stopped for a hot knife each out of the back of an old Post Office van. The hippy in the back really messed us up with a superb hot knife each. We then looked at each other and started to dance as we stumbled into the outer crowds of dancing ravers mixed in with new age travellers.

The bass thudded right through me; you could feel it touch your soul. The music was epic and the DJs could be seen dancing behind the decks. There were indeed topless women, and a lot of them had flowers around their necks and would randomly come up behind you and rub your neck. Everyone was so completely happy and free of all the chains of life and responsibility. Anything you wanted could be purchased from the travellers. The hippy buses and vans had cardboard signs on like 'Veggie burgers £1' or 'aceeeed'. You simply wandered over and bought what you wanted. I had a veggie burger cooked in a filthy pan and then handed to me on an old tin plate. I ate it while sitting on a log by an open fire.

Being stoned, food always tastes good and every greasy mouthful of this charred delight sent signals of pure, culinary pleasure to my brain. Jeff and Nash bought trips and we took our tops off and danced until dawn; oh, the music was so fine. We screamed until we lost our voices and it was like a surreal dream as the sun started to rise. About 8am we found a hippy we knew from Portsdown Hill called Jhohan. He had trundled all the way there and said it had taken him about eight hours and asked if he could have a smoke. We stopped for a spliff and a chat and then set about walking back to the car.

The police had opened the A3 to let the early morning traffic use the road. Every step back to the car was agony; my feet were raw from all the walking and dancing. To add to the torture, Nash and Jeff decided to take another trip, so they were completely off their tits by the time we eventually made it back to my car. That trip back to the car felt like the incredible journey. It seemed to go on forever. You had to think about each and every step and try to cope with the throbbing pain in your shins and feet.

I was so tired that I was in no fit state to drive so Jeff drove us home in my car while he was stoned, drunk and now high as a kite on his second trip. It was nearly midday when I fell through the door at home. And the second my head hit the pillow, I was out like a light. That evening I told my close group of friends what had happened. I was no longer a wannabe but an actual come-of-age raver. It made me so proud. I talked about this for weeks and it has stayed with me forever in the same league as the first time I ever made love.

We then heard of a rave club called Sterns in Worthing. It was known as the House on the Hill. It had been a derelict mansion that had been turned into a massive rave venue. We found some flyers for it in Razzle Records in The Tricorn in Portsmouth. It was a legendary place, almost like a pilgrimage landmark for the raving community born from local legend and tales of supercharged rave music delivered through the latest turbo-charged sound systems.

The flyers were really collectable and all had great pictures on them, normally versions of well-known brands with a raving twist added in like Marmite, Prudential, Quavers and so on. We used to stick them to our walls and dream about going. We also used them for plentiful supplies of roach material, as they were just the right thickness - almost like someone had printed them with that in mind. And they were also cut up and folded into the cases of our mix tapes. One Saturday we decided we would go.

The night was called Bon Voyage and was on Saturday the 6th July 1991. It was a send-off for the DJs who were going to

Ibiza. It had a great line up of DJs including Carl Cox, Colin Dale, Grooverider and Mr C. We had listened over and over again to their mix tapes but never actually seen them perform live. I drove and Gal map read. Well, he was meant to but unfortunately he had used half of the map as roach material for spliffs on the way. So the journey was an ordeal in a blue 2.3 Ghia Sierra that I had borrowed from work. Halfway there I completely lost it as everyone got so stoned they failed to notice that the centre of the rear seat was smouldering and almost on fire. Swain had thrown a spliff out the window and it had blown back in. He was sitting next to it like a dummy while I could see the acrid smoke rising upwards in the rear view mirror.

When we eventually found Highdown Hill, where Sterns was, we could not believe our eyes. It was impressively situated on the top of a large hill, there was a sign hanging in a metal frame over the drive that showed an iconic picture with Sterns written over it. There was no doubt in our mind that we had arrived. Here it was, an impressive old manor house that sat imposingly on top of this hill, surrounded by wonderful gardens. We drove up the hill and the house seemed to get bigger and bigger. As we parked the car we could see people parking and queuing up outside. There were entertainers juggling balls that were on fire and even people making love in the bushes.

We all had Pre Rave Tension as we joined the queue, and I remember seeing a large neon sign that had Sterns written on it, which was a copy of a London underground sign. It was insanely cool. The queue seemed to stretch forever like a happy snake approaching the door. As we got closer I could hear and feel the bass coming through the walls and the muffled voice of an MC. As we got to the door we were searched for drugs and had to put all of our possessions into small plastic bags that were scrutinised. I honestly thought I was going to faint; I was so anxious and overwhelmed. As I walked past the ticket area, you could feel the wooden floorboards shaking beneath your feet and could barely see two feet in front of your face, due to the thick smoke hanging in the air. I was immediately takenaback at just how friendly everyone was and how many hot looking girls were there.

The house was split into three floors and you entered through the top one. This floor was full of people jumping about to the sound of Techno. It had a bar on the left and a really crisp sound system at the end of the room. The walls were adorned with trippy looking pictures that captured your imagination and were designed to captivate your senses. And there were mannequins hanging off the ceiling as you went down a set of cast iron stairs. Randomly it also still had stuffed animal heads on the walls, perhaps from when it was a stately home.

On the dance floor you could see people, who were topless, holding onto these massive speakers, just bobbing their heads in a completely drug induced coma-like state. These sound systems were about £10K each and you could feel them in the pit of your stomach, as the air was rapidly drawn in and pumped out with the reverberating bass. Several people offered us Ecstasy. Es in the rave years were £25 each and half of one would keep you going for days. The guys bought a couple and split them. They knew I would only smoke pot so never offered me any.

We made our way down the staircase to the middle floor. This floor had big footprints on the floor leading in several directions, along corridors and hallways to rooms with games in or a cinema. There was a long bar opposite a dance floor. Again the walls were adorned with all kinds of trippy pictures and there was seating around the edges of this room, where people sat in groups laughing and joking and moving to the music. On that dance floor was the front half of an old, luminously painted VW Beetle with lasers coming out of the headlights. The DJ sat where the driver would normally sit, and could be seen crafting his set in this odd place. It was certainly not anything that I had seen before or since.

Sterns was absolutely packed and so far, it was not disappointing. In fact, it was everything we had heard it was and more. We stayed on the middle floor for about an hour then moved down a very long, grand staircase into the basement. This staircase was iconic with a large rail down the middle and seemed to go on forever. This led to The Basement, a large room that was originally a WW2 bunker so was buried deep in the infrastructure of the property. The bass down there could almost make your ears bleed. It seemed to bounce around from everywhere and had nowhere to escape in this subterranean bunker. It was certainly making the hairs on the back of my neck stand on end.

All the staff had T-shirts on with apple cores which said Hardcore Security. As we got to the bottom, the room was literally shaking. The flyers used to say The Basement had a £20K turbo sound system in it and to this day, it is the loudest thing I have ever heard in such an enclosed, acoustic space. The walls were mirrored with orange and green luminous shapes drawn on them. There was a piercing multi-coloured laser that danced through the smoke in an angelic way. It was beautiful; it changed colour and drew shapes in the smoke and tunnelled into the crowd. Everyone would jump about and put their hands in the air to look down the sweeping tunnel of the laser; it was truly an epic sight.

This underground bunker was absolutely rammed with people blowing whistles, screaming and dancing, all of them were so happy. Underground in Sterns made you feel like a blood cell in a beating heart as the music throbbed through your body in rhythmic pulses.

Everyone was completely off of their tits holding nothing but a bottle of water as they jumped around and screamed as each of the records dropped. The DJs' records slipped seamlessly into each other as they worked the controls on the mixer and the speed of the records. People randomly came up and put Vicks VapoRub on your body or face as apparently it helped you come up if you were on a trip. And it rained sweat in there and when I say rained, I mean rained. It was dripping off the ceiling. One of the MCs on stage kept chanting, "Get wet with sweat." He was spot on.

It was not uncommon for the odd person to pass out at these events. When this happened there would be a cheer as they were lifted up and passed overhead by the ravers towards security. The first few times I watched this I thought it was a bit surreal but after a while it just became normal. The police also raided the place one night and locked everyone in for a while. Deep down I think they just wanted to join in the fun!

I had never seen so many great looking women in one place and a lot of them had virtually nothing on except a bra and pair of leggings so it was really hard to keep your eyes in your head. We danced like never before until the bitter end. I still occasionally dream that I'm at The House on the Hill, in The Basement. I just hope that in the next life, if you get to pick where you end up forever, I would spend eternity living this night over and over again.

I think the weirdest thing was that you could go outside to chill out and skin up and there was an actual Tea Room in the garden that was open all night. You could go in there for a bit of cake and a cuppa that was served to you by some really old dear or another. I have no idea what they must have thought as they gave out cups of tea to hordes of ravers, who'd had far too many drugs. It was surreal!

By the time we left we were all stone deaf and everyone who had been a rave virgin had certainly left their virginity there. It was absolutely awesome. After that night we went as often as we could.

The best nights were put on by a company called In-Ter-Dance. Those nights would become legendary. They were put on by a guy called Mensa. I don't think I ever met him, but he was a legendary party goer by all accounts. His events rocked the South of England until Sterns was closed down by the council because of a massive drug problem. No shit, it had a drug problem? Well the council was right, everyone was off their tits but I would not call it a problem. More of a drug solution than a drug problem as everyone was happy there.

It was a fantastic place and a lot of top DJs and bands made their mark there. Sterns was great in as much as it had a nice garden to chill out in. You walked along a corridor and down some metal stairs to get into it. Often you would just sit on the grass and randomly chat to friendly strangers and pass spliffs around.

The Prodigy played there sometimes. They were just a small but great underground rave music band back then - and a really nice bunch of guys who loved the scene and the music like everyone else did. I'm really pleased they went on to become such legends in their own right. If I had known, a few years later, they would be churning out number ones, I would have at least had my picture taken with them. On another night we watched Moby performing Go and all for the princely sum of £8.

When Sterns closed it left a legendary legacy and a big gap in the heart of the South of England. Sadly, that wonderful promoter Mensa, who used to put on those great In-Ter Dance nights, died in a car accident not long after Sterns closed down. I'm sure if he had still been alive today, In-Ter-Dance would have been as big or even bigger than some of the rave brands that survive today, like Ministry of Sound or Cream. A lot of good things came out of Sterns. This fabulous club rave venue really helped to shape a lot of lives and careers. And for that a lot of people will be eternally grateful. No matter how heartfelt I write my Sterns experiences, I fear that unless you lived it, I will never be able to do the House on the Hill justice.

I spent the whole of the rave years stoned practically every day; we all did. The first thing you did in the morning and last thing you did at night was have a spliff. Life revolved around being stoned and raving.

Another great rave was Treasure Island, an outdoor gig held on 17th August 1991 at Golden Hill Fort on the Isle of Wight. It had a great DJ line-up and we had all excitedly bought tickets. The weather was great, it was a shorts and T-shirt day. We all headed to the ferry and when we arrived on the island, a double decker bus had been laid on to collect ravers and take them to the Fort. Golden Hill Fort looked like a Victorian redbrick structure that stretched around an open courtyard, where the sound system was located. The DJs and MCs were up on a balcony overlooking the event. The sound system was a massive £25K rig and as you got nearer, it felt like your bones were rattling inside your body and you could feel the bass in your stomach. I'm sure my raving days were partly responsible for my tinnitus in later life!

As the sun went down we enjoyed walking on the ramparts and stomping in the courtyard, to the latest and greatest rave tunes. I always remember that Scabby Jake, famous for his one and only frog covered top, had taken a couple of Ecstasy pills and was jumping about like a mad thing. The rest of the guys were also on planet 'E' except for me. I was stoned but that was it. Around midnight it got very cold. All of us only had the shorts and T-shirts we were wearing and there was nowhere to get warm. So we decided to dance non-stop to keep warm.

Swain's little brother was absolutely wasted and was stomping about, grinning from ear to ear. How he managed to stay upright was beyond me. There was an awesome laser show during the night but the smoke dissipated fairly quickly as we were outdoors. I remember almost falling over two people who were screwing each other right in the middle of the dance floor. And the usual drug induced happy, hard-core ravers were out in force. One of them was so out of it he was stood with his head on the sound system for virtually the whole night. I can only imagine the lasting brain damage that must have given him, let alone the ringing in his ears that must have lasted for days afterwards. That's if he had any hearing left.

After 3am the night dragged on as it was so cold. Even dancing all night wasn't enough to keep us warm. But then we were only wearing shorts and T shirts. Finally, the sun came up and you could feel the early morning rays warming up the cold night air. It certainly lifted our spirits and helped get rid of the goose bumps. These kinds of mornings really made you feel glad to be alive; glad to be part of the rave scene and glad to be able to enjoy it with your best friends.

However, by around 6am I was completely spent. I had been jumping around all night on nothing more than a bit of puff and a few beers. I was hungry and there were no buses to shuttle people back to the ferry until after 9am. Most of the other guys were still in the groove and either tripping on acid or ecstasy. I walked out of the Fort and thought I would wait at the bus stop, as I could chill out there. I sat down and shared a spliff with some other people waiting at the bus stop and we got talking. That's the thing about when you went raving, there was never any trouble and everyone was as friendly as your own brothers or sisters.

After chatting for a while it turned out they all lived on the island and one of their mates, whose nickname was Acid Andy, was doing shuttle runs. I explained I had to wait a few more hours for the party bus back to the ferry and they said they would get me a lift. I was really chuffed. About twenty minutes later my lift arrived. Acid Andy certainly lived up to his reputation. He was absolutely off his tits and was driving a yellow three-wheeled van like Del's out of Only Fools and Horses. The only difference was that instead of writing on either side, there was a large Acid Smiley face. The back was covered in purple velour carpet and it had home stereo speakers pumping out rave tunes. About six or seven of us piled in and I watched as he did a line of either speed or coke before we set off. Another passenger asked, "Andy, you still tripping?" to which he replied, "Always," with a massive grin on his face.

Great, so here I was sat in the back of a three-wheeled van, with smileys on either side, driven by Acid Andy, who was tripping and had also just snorted a line of coke or something! I sat there for a split second, weighing up my options and then I thought, "Fuck it, I'm gonna skin up." So I rolled a massive spliff and we passed it around in the van as we set off.

Now I have never been in the back of a three-wheeled van before but Acid Andy must have fancied himself as a three-wheeled world racing champion. We were flying, well in three-wheeled van terms. He ran a red light. Someone had said, "Red light Acid," but he replied. "Don't worry, it's early morning and there's only one copper covering the whole island."

I thought the van was going to roll over. Everyone in the back was getting thrown around and just laughing as we were all stoned. It ended up like being a game of Twister with tangled arms and legs everywhere. There were a couple of girls in the back and I could hear one of them complaining about where someone else's hand had ended up. But then everyone just started laughing as Acid started deliberately weaving the van down a side road; it was hilarious. And being stoned meant you couldn't stop laughing. I have no idea how I arrived safely at the ferry port but somehow I did; thanks to these guys and Acid Andy and his three-wheeled van.

I got the ferry back then drove to Kath's Mum's house in Copnor. I shoved Kath out of bed and fell asleep for the rest of the day. It would have been a perfect plan if I hadn't have told Kath I couldn't see her the night before because I was working late. Oops!

Chapter Twelve
Hot Knives

I had a lovely 1976 silver VW Scirocco, that I bought from work. I can still remember the registration and every tiny detail about it. The car was like a kid's dream come true. It was fairly fast and I used to drive it around on work's trade insurance policy. Despite its age the car shifted and was reliably German. We used to go everywhere in this car. Quite often we would park up in the country and do hot knives or smoke spliffs, if we couldn't be bothered to skin up.

I was working hard and doing long hours at the garage. One Saturday night I was looking forward to going to Port Road for a smoke with Dale, who by now was in the navy, Fizz and a friend off the Reservation called Francis. Francis had recently joined the army and on the way down in the car, he kept saying the army was better than the navy. They got onto the subject of who could drink more, sailors or squaddies and so on.

When we arrived at Port Road everyone was doing hot knives. As I said earlier, a hot knife is exactly what it sounds like. Two knives would be heated up on a stove until glowing red, then underneath a large plastic bottle they would be pressed together with some puff in-between. You would pick up the puff by dabbing it with one knife and then quickly turn it over and squash down on it with the other hot knife. It got you stoned really fast as you inhaled the thick pure smoke through the top of a large Ribena bottle with the bottom cut away so no smoke could escape.

After a few you would either be mega hyperactive or a complete slobbering wreck.; depending on the particular puff you were smoking. Dale and Francis decided to settle the who could drink more debate that had been going on in the car. Before they headed out into Cosham they both had a couple of hot knives so they were well on their way. It was a fairly typical night at Port Road. We listened to loud rave music and talked about raves, DJs and women. The normal kind of crap that was immensely interesting only when you are stoned, in a bubble with your friends.

I remember going to get two pizzas from the high street. Aside from the other things cannabis does to you, it has a 'way out west' effect on your brain regarding food. It makes you really hungry and you get the The Munchies but every mouthful tastes like you are eating Adam and Eve's apple. It is truly divine, better than divine. In fact, it's like tasting food in 3D on a whole other level and makes you truly believe you have never actually tasted food before. We all sat there eating this pizza and grunting about how good it was. In actual fact it was probably disgusting but when you're stoned it tastes epic.

The doorbell rang. It was Dale and Francis and they were steaming drunk, and I mean steaming drunk. I'm not even sure how they got back from the pub. Dale looked at Francis and said, "knives," meaning hot knives. And looked at me to do them. I really didn't want to as I was enjoying my pizza so much; it was good sex to my taste buds. But they kept on and on about it, so begrudgingly I stuck about two smokes worth on each knife. They had about three each and were still going on about the army/navy thing in a slurred manner. As they inhaled the thick smoke through the bottle, I noticed the knives had been burning the plastic as well, so they were inhaling a mixture of melting plastic fumes along with large servings of pot on top of a shit ton of alcohol. Plus, the knives from earlier. They had a few more drinks before entering some 'mong out phase.' The mong out phase is when you are so nailed you just want to lie down or can't move.

Me and Fizz somehow managed to get them in the back of the car for the journey home over Portsdown Hill. It was kind of like having two bodies in the back of the car. They were slumped against each other in a complete state. Just as we were going up the Hill, without warning, Francis threw up everywhere and was unable to even try to put his hand over his mouth or speak. He never even raised his arms and looked as if nobody was at home. I looked in the rear view mirror to see vomit all over Dale who was just sitting there. He too was hardly able to speak or move. And then he started throwing up all over himself.

By the time we pulled up at Fort Nelson viewpoint there must have been about twenty pints of sick everywhere. Now I know reading this you are thinking yeah, right, but trust me, it was everywhere and everything they had both drunk that night was spattered all over the car. And because neither of them could stop the other being sick on them, it was like some awful chain reaction. My car was a three-door coupe, which meant there were no windows in the back to get any air in or for them to be sick out of. They were both trapped in this hideous vomit fest.

After initially screaming his head off, Dale just sat there in a vegetative state and threw up over and over, stopping only briefly for breath before continuing. Me and Fizz wound down the front windows and stuck our heads out while this was going on. I had been desperate to get to Fort Nelson as quick as I could. When we got there I skidded up and jammed the handbrake on at the same time as we flung the doors open and bailed out. Dale and Francis were both still stuck in the back of the car and you could see sick covered hands moving on the inside of the rear windows and hear muffled screams for help.

Fizz and I were both getting our breath back and bent down to take in the cool, clean air. We discussed what to do. We covered our noses and looked in the car. We needed to get them out and try to straighten them up a bit. Fizz pushed the passenger seat forward so he could reach in and try and grab Dale by his arm. He had to try several times as Dale was covered in sick and it was making him gag. Somehow Fizz managed to drag the dead weight out of the car, onto the grass. I had to do the same with Francis.

It was disgusting and I'm pretty sure at least one of them had soiled themselves. The smell was terrible and every time you moved them they threw up. In a kind of triage way, we decided the best thing we could do to help us get a grip on the situation was to skin up. We rummaged through Dale's pockets for the puff and the skins and while we were doing it, he piped up, "Stop stealing my puff you bastards," in a slurred voice. But he was physically helpless to do anything. Dale had lost all use of his limbs.

While we were having a smoke we could see that Francis had

somehow managed to get to his feet briefly and was now throwing up down the side and across the bonnet of the car. He fell onto his knees and crawled a short way off, groaning to himself. Dale, on the other hand, was worryingly lifeless. He was totally and completely unresponsive now. We were sure he was dead or at the very least about to die. We were slapping Dale's face, calling his name and shaking him but we got nothing at all. I started to scream, "He's fucking dead, he's fucking dead. Shit, what are we going to do?" We said we would leave Francis lying on the grass and come back later for him. We would try to get Dale to the nearby Queen Alexandra hospital.

Then one of us came up with the idea of turning him onto his side and hitting him on the back. As we did this Dale took a massive gasp for breath. He was still unconscious but the sick he had been choking on had cleared and he started to breathe again. Unquestionably this move saved his life. I have honestly never been so frightened or relieved in my whole life. I was sure he was a goner. These guys had sunk copious amounts of drink; beer, spirits, then those double hot knives. I have never ever to this day seen anyone so messed up. And because I had done the hot knives for them, it made the hairs on the back of my neck stand up as I knew if Dale died, I would be at least partly responsible.

After about an hour Dale was barely conscious but it was a great relief. We discussed leaving them both there overnight to sleep it off, now the danger seemed to have passed. But we knew deep down we needed to get them home. It was terrible; we needed to get the half dead back into the rear seats without them being sick everywhere again or us being sick. Fortunately, they were both in this kind of semi-comatose, zombie state by now, as we had been there for several hours. Whilst Dale and Francis couldn't stand or function unassisted, they did have a few basic cognitive movements that could be used to get them back in the car, if we assisted and shouted instructions. It must have taken about an hour to load them into the back of the car. The smell was disgusting even with the front windows open. Finally, we set off.

It was the break of dawn by the time we got to Dale's house. We parked and pulled him out of the car and assisted him to his front door. I got his keys and opened the door while Fizz held him up. After the door was opened we gave him a little help by gently pushing him through. He managed to take about two steps before we heard the thud of him falling to the floor. We threw his keys in the hallway, along with him and closed the door. After we got Francis out of the car, he managed to get to his door under his own steam. So all in all I would say it was definitely squaddies who could take more!

By the time I dropped Fizz off I was so tired that when I got home I was out like a light as soon as my head touched the pillow. I woke up about 2pm. It was a lovely hot day and the mid-afternoon heat hit me as I walked out the door. My car was parked on the green outside the house. I must have navigated the pedestrian bollards the night before as you couldn't get a car up there normally. The car was covered in rock hard sick that had been baked on by the sun. And there were flies buzzing around; it was disgusting.

I opened the door at arm's length and the smell hit me and I took several steps back. The true horrors of the night before were all there for me to try to deal with. There was even sick on the roof lining. It was everywhere and at least one of them had been on the Snakebite and Black. I ended up taking the whole interior out and hosing it off in the garden as it was so bad. Probably one of the most hideous things I have ever had to do.

Normally when you buy a car you have a few driving lessons first. Cotton on the other hand had bought a white Ford Cortina car while he was working as a kitchen porter locally. I must say I was somewhat surprised to see him purchase a car. He never actually seemed that fussed about driving and seemed to enjoy either walking or taking the bus. One day he came to my door with a beaming smile on his face. "Monty, guess who bought a car? Can you teach me to drive?" I asked him where it was and he said it needed picking up from two or three miles away. So I offered to give him a lift. And Kath came too.

While we were driving over there I asked, "How you gonna get it home?" He replied, "It can't be that hard, you do it," and laughed. Then he said, "Don't worry, I'm a professional." It was something Cotton often said, just before he was about to get caught shoplifting or doing a burglary. It never filled me with much confidence. A rough translation should have been something like, "Get ready, this is going to be messy." Whenever he said it, Kath and I used to look at each other and that look said it all.

The car was on a road with two or three shops on it. It was fairly close to the church cemetery where we used to play 'Murderer in the Dark.' Cotton hopped out of the car and then jumped into his. It goes without saying that he had no insurance, tax, MOT, L plates or even a driving licence. This was the Reservation way of doing things. It was assumed that if you owned the car it was legal because you weren't driving a stolen car. The other bits were optional and should not be viewed as an obstacle to your entitlement to be on the road.

I told Cotton, "Follow me, let's go to the Heath." He grinned excitedly through his open window. As I was turning my car around, I witnessed something completely unrelated and very strange. Just in front of us was an argument going on between two guys in a white Ford Fiesta. Someone in a shell suit was standing on the pavement, pointing and shouting through the passenger window of the car. It was most probably a drug deal gone bad but the pedestrian was extremely agitated and getting more and more abusive. He then started hitting the passenger in the face over and over again, in a blind rage.

Then I saw something that belonged in a cartoon or Hollywood movie. The passenger in the car grabbed the furious pedestrian's hand and wound the window up, trapping him and his hand. Then they tried starting the car which seemed to be taking forever. Meanwhile the pedestrian was hitting the glass with his spare hand, trying to escape. Finally, the car started and they proceeded to drive down the road, with the even more annoyed pedestrian running alongside screaming. He started out at a jogging speed but was soon breaking the four-minute mile. Then, when his legs could go no faster, he fell but they continued to drag his screaming and kicking body alongside the car. It was only 50 yards or so later that they opened the window enough to let him fall to the ground. I remember thinking that guy must have a severe case of 'gravel rash'. And although I felt his pain, I couldn't stop laughing; after all it was comical. But it did go to show just how random everyday events could be on the Reservation.

I looked in the rear view mirror just in time to see Cotton turn the corner behind me. It was clear he was stuck in first gear, bouncing along at about 30 mph. The car was screaming and the engine sounded like it was about to blow up. As Cotton went round a corner he turned far too hard and far too early. I watched in disbelief as he wedged the rear of the Cortina into a red Ford Escort parked near the corner. But Cotton kept his foot on the accelerator until he managed to drive off.

I'm afraid that despite the serious nature of the situation, Kath and I were killing ourselves laughing as we pulled over to wait for him. We were about a mile or so away from the car park when we pulled over to let a bus through. But Cotton, who really couldn't drive, just carried on and tried to fit through the gap with the bus. It was far too narrow. All you could hear was this loud scraping sound as Cotton scraped the side of the car. This short drive was rapidly turning into what can only be described as roadside 'banger racing'. This was the second accident he'd had in barely two minutes. Again we couldn't help but laugh as he blindly carried on, still in first gear.

On the final part of the journey Cotton had to navigate a roundabout on a main road and turn right across a busy junction. He was still behind us and we were expecting another accident but by the grace of God he somehow managed to get to the Heath car park in one piece, despite still being in first gear, and bunny hopping the entire way. When he pulled up beside us he wound down the window and said, "I told you I was a professional," and laughed. I said, "Yeah, a professional dick by all accounts. What about the Escort and the bus?" But Cotton just laughed and said, "Skin up Mart." But I said no. "We need to get your car moved in case the police are looking for you." So I parked mine and hopped in with Kath and drove Cotton's car further out into the country. I drove it through a road known as Dead Man's Corner and then through a local ford, that was filled with about a foot or so of water. I parked the car on a layby at the bottom of Portsdown Hill, under some oak trees on Scratchface Lane. Cotton was still buzzing about his first driving experience and kept pestering me to skin up.

So here seemed as good a place as any to have a spliff and we all sat there laughing about his shocking professional driving. The mood was really light and now we all had the giggles. I said: "Right Cotton, this is what you need to do.

"Basically stick it in first gear and rev it up as high as it goes, and then let your foot off the clutch as fast as you can. Then, when it won't rev up any further, change gear by banging the clutch down and throwing it into second. Don't bother taking your foot off the gas, it will be smoother."

Surely anyone would know this was a joke? But instead, Cotton said, "Cool. You coming then?" as he hopped into the driver's seat. I looked at Kath and could see there was no way either of us wanted to be in that car when he was driving. So I replied, "No mate, we will watch from here."

So Cotton wound the window down and revved up the car as much as it would go. I had the stoned giggles and shouted, "That's it mate, now let the clutch out as fast as you can." In an instant, as he released the clutch, the car wheels spun and he skidded off like he was competing in the Le Mans 24 Hour Race. He was struggling to keep control while we were left literally choking in the dust cloud as he tore up the surface of the dusty layby and sped off. Again we both couldn't help laughing as we watched him erratically speed off and heard the car scream as Cotton abruptly changed into second gear.

We waited for about twenty minutes but he still wasn't back. Then, all of a sudden we could hear an over revving car coming around the corner. Sure enough, there was Cotton grinning like a Cheshire cat… and erratically steering his speeding death trap towards Kath and me. As we ran for cover, I noticed that the car was now missing its front bumper and was dragging a fairly large branch along with it. I have to say it was hilarious; what on earth had he been up to? "Oh, that? I'm a professional you know. Must have been where I turned around."

The car now resembled a proper 'banger racing' car. Both sides were scraped and it had sticks and vegetation poking out of it. This thing was virtually trashed. We had another spliff and then Cotton offered to drive us back to our car. I have no idea quite why but we said we'd prefer to walk! Kath and I watched as he spun away towards the top of Portsdown Hill. Again we were covered in a cloud of dust.

The next time we met up Cotton said he'd broken down in a country lane, later that day. And when he went to collect the car, a week or so later, a farmer had shot it to bits. All the windows were smashed and the car was riddled with shotgun pellet holes so he left it there. I thought it was probably a blessing in disguise. Not being behind the wheel might have saved his life or someone else's. I don't think to this day Cotton drives and I can honestly say it's probably best for mankind, after seeing first hand his 'professional driving' that day.

Cars played an important role on the Reservation. I remember one night being out in the Renault. As I was looking for a parking space I noticed about ten or so of my friends up Portsdown Hill. I pulled up and joined them. We chatted as we skinned up. When I looked around there was only one other car. It was driven by a friend called Mike and was a skip of a Renault 11 and when I say skip I mean skip - a real mess. It turned out that the whole lot of them had been in the one car. After everyone had had a smoke and jumped about a bit on the grass, they set about leaving. I remember watching in disbelief as two people were shut in the boot. Only moments before they were fighting about who would have to go in there. The pair were laughing, screaming, and banging as the boot lid was closed. Then about four other people squeezed onto the back seat and a few more sat on their laps. I watched as this skip of a car tried to move. This green, rust bucket looked like some kind of low rider, scraping along the floor and the wheels sitting deeply into the wheel arches.

This car was a common sight in and around the Reservation. Mike used to drive it like a complete dick. I mean everyone was either stoned or pissed but Mike used to throw it about. And it was often overloaded with human cargo, all packed in like sardines. One night the same idiot tried ramming and racing me through Purbrook Heath. Again it was fully loaded with at least ten people. Mike was clearly stoned and somehow chased me and my friends in my car for several miles. It was quite funny but at the same time quite scary. We drove through a river, over speed bumps, along dirt tracks and ended up on the top of Portsdown Hill again.

Mike skidded up onto the grass next to me and I could hear the groaning of all of the poor souls he had in the car. About six or seven came out of the back seat and then the unlucky ones in the boot could be heard screaming and banging. They really had drawn the short straw as I can only imagine the pain and discomfort they had just experienced. And no one seemed at all bothered about opening the boot and letting them out. I asked, "Aren't you going to let them out?" Everyone laughed and said, "No, it' s still their turn." And sure enough, we were there for at least half an hour, jumping about on the grass to loud rave music and having a smoke. Meanwhile those poor souls could be heard protesting at being stuck in the boot before we shot off again, with the Renault in hot pursuit. To this day I don't know who those two were, stuck in the boot, but I expect they've had better nights out.

Another night, while I was out in my Renault, I was pulled over by the police. I never had any insurance and we were all stoned so the car was full of smoke. It was like a hot box so getting away with something like this was always a matter of charm with the police. I had been pulled over for having a rear light out. Dale was sat right behind me as the blues and twos came on. He was midway through skinning up a spliff as I pulled over. I was really panicking and said, "Get rid of it for God's sake." I got out of the car and spoke to the policeman, who pointed out that I had a faulty tail light and that was basically it.

He asked everyone to get out of the car so my friends were all standing on the grass next to the pavement. Dale was the quietest I had ever seen him. It was only after the copper left that I looked at him and watched as he spat out a load of tobacco. In his infinite wisdom he had decided to eat the spliff; not throw it out the window or hide it in the car but simply eat it.

"What if the officer had asked you something?"

"I would have pretended to be mute."

"Right, so there's me driving along with my mute mate called Dale, listening to rave music in a hot boxed car?" That one was hardly going to fly was it? Completely unbelievable!

A little later we stopped in a car park in Purbrook Heath. Cotton was in the back and it was the first time he had smoked pot. We sat in the car laughing and talking for an hour or so and listening to a rave tape. I asked Cotton, "Are you stoned? How does it feel?" He replied it had done absolutely nothing to him and he had no idea what all the fuss was about.

I then said: "Fair enough, ok, let's go. Cotton can you close the door?"

"I can't," he said.

I asked why and he replied: "I can't move my head." It was hilarious, he honestly believed he couldn't move his head.

A few weeks later everyone was experimenting with Acid. I never did as I'd heard so many bad things about it. But somehow Cotton, who had only just popped his stoner cherry had been talked into taking a trip. Swain used to try and freak people out on their first trips so took great enjoyment from Cotton taking a Microdot Trip. I did tell him not to but peer pressure had got to him. Well, as everyone was coming up we ended up at Paulsgrove

Chalk Cliffs. I'm trying to think of how exactly to describe this. If you imagine a sheer rock face made out of chalk, that was several hundred feet high, with some really narrow small ledges on which you could skilfully navigate upwards, that would be a start. I believe all the chalk was mined to use under the motorway when they built the M27 in the 60s. Anyway we ended up here and climbed up these sheer cliffs while everyone was stoned and most people were tripping. Poor old Cotton came up on his trip as he was about half way up the cliffs. I can honestly say that how we all managed to get back down without any serious accidents was a miracle.

Acid was really bad. I watched them all go nuts as they tripped and came up. I can honestly say it's not something that I ever wanted to do. I sat there thinking where this drugs thing had started and where it was going to end. It went back to Swain and Scabby Jake at school, when they wanted to try Magic Mushrooms really badly. One night they picked half a carrier bag full from the school playing field and brewed it up into tea. Afterwards we all assumed they must have been on a massive trip as they had been off school for a few days. Well it turns out that the idiots had only gone and eaten half a bag full of poisonous toad stools. Seriously they could have killed themselves twice over, they were very lucky.

Locally, everyone was fully aware of the effects of taking Acid. There was a local lad called Jif. I knew him but he was not a close friend of mine. Well he was bang into popping trips up on Portsdown Hill. One night he did a trip near a cave in the chalk face, adjacent to the viewpoint and he never came down. It had somehow short-wired his brain. Jif burnt all his clothes and stole a bike and rode home in the nude. He ended up getting sectioned and several years later we bumped into him and asked, "How are you Jif? How did you get out and are you ok now?" He just looked at us and pulled a spoon out of his pocket and said, "I broke out with this spoon," and just carried on walking, with a thousand-yard stare. That was the last time I ever laid eyes on him. I often wonder if he ever did make a recovery.

As the recession dug deeper and deeper and poor credit finance became more prevalent, the garage sold fewer and fewer cars. I would go to increasing lengths to close a deal. I took one customer out on L-plates and yes, you've guessed it, he wrote off the car with me in it. I have no idea how but Colin got him to pay for the car. I was a bit shaken but seriously, L-plates on a test drive? It was a disaster waiting to happen.

Another time one of the rusty wrecks, a 1978 Ford Fiesta, was painted so it looked pretty but was actually full of filler. While going down the motorway the guy on the test drive opened the driver's window. Unfortunately, this meant there was an increase in pressure in the car which blew the rear window right out of the car, as the rust and filler gave way. It flew out like the ejector seat of an aircraft. One minute it was there, the next it had flown out the back.

Unfortunately, the recession in the early 90s and Colin's wife's ill-health meant the garage went bankrupt and Colin had to shut up shop. The bank had foreclosed and he had to vacate both the showroom and the garage. He asked Pete and I to burn all the paperwork, receipts, invoices etc. Basically anything that could prove he had ever been trading. We loaded all the paperwork into a massive square, metal box in the yard. It was spitting rain, as it was late autumn, so rather damp. I tried lighting the box but it just kept going out. Pete came back with a can of petrol and said, "Let me have a go." He threw the whole can over the paperwork and then bent over it to light it. The second his thumb struck the lighter there was an almighty explosion. I watched in disbelief as he was thrown backwards onto the floor and landed in the wet mud.

I remember thinking how lucky he was but what an idiot he had been. When he stopped rubbing his black face I could see that all his eyebrows, lashes and a large part of his hair had been singed clean off. Pete looked like a chicken leg that had been thrown into the flames on a BBQ and flash fried. He was fine as he had no actual burns to the skin because it had been a flash explosion but he was bald as a baby's backside. He went to get cleaned up and I could hear him screaming as he looked at his almost hairless head and blackened face.

My time at Colin's was physically hard work and often mentally and morally challenging but I have to say I really enjoyed it. Working there made me feel a lot more confident. I was like a sponge and soaked up what I could about business and commerce. Well the good bits at least! But my time there was certainly character building and you could write an entire book about those experiences alone.

Colin had so much confidence, was excellent on the phone, great with people, knew how to negotiate and was driven. I absorbed every bit I could and even today, there is a lot of Colin in me and I owe him so much.

The Reservation

Chapter Thirteen
The Tripper

My room at home was an odd space. It basically looked like someone had tipped a skip load of rubbish upside down over the floor. And this rubbish consisted of empty beer cans, wine bottles, crisp packets and lots and lots of clothes. Because I used to work at the garage, clothes often had an oily smell. I used to work long days and generally go for a drink with my boss. So by the time I got home I was normally half cut and just rolled into bed, if I wasn't seeing Kath.

On the bedroom wall my friends and I had sprayed a massive mural of the world. It was actually pretty good and had pictures of cool looking spray cans in each corner, all leaning towards the centre of the mural. And there was a break in the ozone layer over the North Pole with the slogan 'leave the ozone alone'. We had all proudly tagged it. But seriously though, we had actually sprayed this on the wall to remind us that spray cans ruined the ozone layer? Definitely not one of my brightest ideas.

My tag was Exit and I sprayed it everywhere. At school I had drawn it all over my books, desk and lockers. At our 10-year school reunion a former classmate pointed out one of my tags on an old locker. A fitting memorial to the time I spent there. My Mum wasn't particularly pleased with the graffiti on my bedroom wall but after a while she came to accept it. I was also the proud owner of a two-belt drive Pioneer turntable from the 70s that I'd bought cheap. These things were awesome; they were one of the first set of decks on the Reservation. We used to get stoned and mix rave tracks together, really badly. But hey, sometimes when you are nutted it was quite pleasing. These were the first set of decks that a lot of us ever used. And one thing that became compulsory to master on the Reservation, over the next few years, was mixing. Pretty much everyone on the Reservation ended up able to mix to a fairly decent standard. I guess a set of decks was equivalent to a flute or recorder in more affluent areas.

A few of my friends went on to DJ at a fairly high level and even today the Incredible Bullshitting man (Neil) plays or MCs at Oldskool nights. Another one of my friends even had a top ten record. My neighbours must have loved us when we were in my room with the decks. Either that or they acquired a new love for all things rave.

One of my most precious possessions, when growing up, was a poster and to this day it's tattooed on my brain. Especially as it proved to be one of the most inspirational items I have ever owned. When I was about fourteen my brother Mark gave it to me; well he left it on the wall when he moved out which is kind of the same thing. It was like a rite of passage for me, moving into the larger bedroom and it came with this wonderful poster. It was a beautiful blonde woman with long, curly hair in a bikini, leaning across a red Porsche 911 Turbo. She had a pair of reflective Aviator sunglasses on and had a very contented and loving look on her face. This poster was the last thing I looked at before I went to bed and the first thing I woke up to in the morning. I used to look at her and that Porsche and dream that one day I would own a Porsche and have a nice woman to go with it.

When it was really cold you could see your breath in my bedroom but thanks to the warm sunlight on her tanned skin, the poster somehow kept the cold out. Day in day out I dreamt about owning a Porsche one day and vowed that I would make my dream come true. My goal was so real that it set me on the path to chasing my dreams for the rest of my life. I don't know what happened to that poster, but to this day I wish I still had it. I have spent countless hours trying to find a copy but never have. There were probably thousands of 80s Porsche posters printed so the odds should be good but no luck so far. We always used to enjoy a spliff before going to sleep. It used to help send you off to sleep in a great way. When you smoke pot you can smell it a mile off.

I also had a couple of chipmunks in my bedroom. They used to climb the curtains and drink leftover wine in the bottom of glasses. Kath loved animals and they were really cute. While one died of old age, I'm not quite sure what happened to the other one. One day, while Kath and I were out, someone had been in my room and left the door open. Monty went missing, never to be seen again. We were both devastated but decided not to get another one as it could happen again. I think our cat FC probably ate Monty.

While I was working at Cheap Wheels I bought an MK1 Mexico Escort from two guys called the Dishonest Brothers who lived in Paulsgrove for £125. This car only got me to the top of Portsdown Hill before it broke down on the way home. Clearly nothing from the Dishonest Brothers came with any kind of warranty so I was screwed. When we went to tow it home the next day, it had already been half stripped. Then, after a few weeks parked outside my house, there was even less of it left. To cut a long story short one of my neighbours asked if I wanted to swap it for an A4 envelope full of weed. I jumped for joy and nearly ripped his arm off. I figured that if the car stayed out there much longer, there would be either hardly anything left or the car would be gone. We were smoking this weed like it was going out of fashion. But after a week we were fed up of the stuff. It stank and was far smellier than the usual resin we smoked. The smell hung in the air and even with the window open I wondered why my Mum never asked me what it was.

One night Kath and I came home and the minute I stuck the key in the door and opened it, you could smell that weed hanging in the air. I looked at Kath and she looked at me and said, "Shit, what's going on here?" My Mum then shouted, "Heeeeeelo." As we walked into the lounge our worst fears came true. Mum was sitting there with a grin on her face wider than a Cheshire cat's. "Martin, I rolled up all your cigarette ends as I didn't have any fags." My heart sank as it dawned on me that my Mum was absolutely nutted on this skunk weed that was in our ashtray by the bed.

Then she said, "I was ironing and the day has gone really slowly," and, "I have made a stew and it's lovely." And started laughing, uncontrollably. When she mentioned the stew I knew she must have had The Munchies as her cooking was terrible. And no one ever said, in the history of mankind, that they liked her food; even the local cats, dogs and foxes would leave it. Then

Mum asked what was in these cigarette ends??? Now for a split second I thought of replying, "Nothing." But she was so 'nutted' and unusually happy that I came clean and said she had been smoking pot. She took it surprisingly well and just kept laughing all night.

Over the coming months she used to enjoy having the odd smoke with us and my friends when they came round. Even to this day it all sounds a bit surreal. It was kind of cool that now there was no reason to hide the fact we smoked it. But sitting in the lounge with my mates and passing my Mum a spliff was still kind of weird. She was entering our own little bubble and our private space, this cool, secret underground thing we did now had its lid blown off. I think in a lot of ways it was actually quite character building for Mum. But for me it was just weird but at least she was happy and very funny. Mum soon got fed up with it so it ended up being cool again! And she never did go through our dog ends again.

After Cheap Wheels I started selling cars on my own. It was the same sort of stuff I had been doing at the garage. I would buy them in local papers or at local auctions, then clean them up and polish some value into them. It was altogether a riskier business on your own, as I didn't have a lot of capital so every time I bought a car, if it went wrong, it could wipe me out financially. It was lonely work too as I had a small council lock-up that I rented about a mile from home.

But as I started to sell a few cars my confidence grew and I was able to invest the profits into essentials that I needed like tools and spray gear. It was a fairly big gamble buying all of this stuff but I really did need it to move forward. I gambled every penny I had on this gear and a metallic blue Vauxhall Cavalier. The car was pretty okay and had come from Portsmouth Car Auctions. I took it to the lock-up only to discover that everything I had just bought had been stolen; all my tools my paint gear, everything. The garage was completely cleaned out. My heart sank. Everything I had worked so hard for. This gear represented every penny I had along with the car.

Dragging my feet along despondently I got back into the car I had just bought and screamed "Fuck," while hitting the steering wheel. I realised that it would probably take me months to build up enough cash to buy the gear all over again. I spoke to Kath about what had happened and she was pretty supportive. But we both knew I was sunk when it came to selling cars. I had bills to pay and would probably have to sell the Cavalier. And now I couldn't carry out any repairs. I might make a few quid but not enough to keep my original capital. But I figured it would be great to give the car a run over the weekend before I tried to sell it.

I bumped into someone in Waterlooville who told me about another 'spiral tribe' rave, similar to the awesome one I had been to a few years earlier. This time it was being held in Winchester near a power plant. It hadn't started well. The night before we had followed a convoy that had split into several parts due to harassment by the police. We arrived at a different site to the one where it was actually going down. There were lots of new age travellers and part of a stage was on this site so we thought this must be the main site. The only problem was we had brought Neil with us. As soon as we got there he assumed the rave would go down and he bought two trips off a hippy. Rather than waiting until things went down, he decided to drop them both so he was in full swing as soon as the sound gear turned up.

Well, the police seized the lorry with the sound equipment. So after having a chat with a few hippies and listening to some music with the car doors open we decided to go home. Neil was buzzing and would not shut up, no matter what. He was running his hands in front of his face and rapping to himself, while stopping now and then to scream. It was really weird.

He asked us to drop him about two or three miles from home as he was going to go for a trundle. It was 3am but I thought okay, he should be alright. So we let him out of the car and went home to bed. On the Saturday night we headed up again and passed Neil on the side of the road. I stopped and asked, "Are you ok man? Gonna come back up with us?" But he said, "No man, I'm trundling still." So I drove off.

Kath and I joined a convoy with some of the other locals. After the drive there we parked up and could immediately see several sound systems and floods and floods of people flocking to the area by foot. You could tell straight off the bat that this was going to be one hell of an event. It was the epitome of a free festival. The massive party vibe and the intrinsic, rhythmic thud of the rave music heightened all of your senses.

As we got closer we could see the silhouettes of people on top of a hill with the lights and lasers flashing behind them. I remember thinking that I was a part of something really special. The sights and sounds, and every beat of the music seemed to engulf me over and over again. I stood there dancing and waving my hands in the air when something completely overpowered me. I couldn't take a breath and fell to my knees onto the soft grass. In the moments that followed the feelings of love, music and life were replaced by those of anxiety and a longing to get away.

I screamed for Kath and begged her to help me get some help. We were faced with the daunting task of trying to get some help in the middle of an illegal rave at night. Thousands of party goers were almost treading on me as they jumped about. Kath helped me up and told me to put my arm around her. I gasped for breath as she helped me towards a road we had passed that had a lot of police on. It felt like an eternity to get there. My feet were stumbling and dragging along the floor and my legs felt heavy like I was wearing lead boots. I might as well have been trying to ascend Everest as each breath was laboured and I felt as if no oxygen was getting into my lungs. Eventually we reached the road and asked the police for help. A female officer could clearly see I was in distress and used her radio to call for an ambulance.

As we waited on the side of the kerb I was squeezing Kath's hand so tightly that I remember her screaming. Then I started to grab her leg and again my grip was so hard that it hurt her. I was in a real state by now and going into shock and shaking. What was happening to me? When the ambulance arrived the paramedics looked at me and decided to take me to Winchester Accident and Emergency. I remember being in a cubicle while the doctors and nurses discussed what they thought was wrong with me. I heard one of them say, "He is one of those druggy ravers that are at that local, big illegal party. He's probably having an adverse effect to Ecstasy." I really did not like being referred to like this. Yes, I smoked pot and liked a drink but that was it, I felt like I had been judged and would now be treated like some kind of drug addict.

After the doctors looked at me they did think I had taken Ecstasy as my heart rate was racing. But as I had some unusual symptoms he thought I was having some kind of severe anxiety attack. At this point the penny dropped. One of those slimy scum bag, so called friends of mine had given me an open bottle of beer which I drank as we were walking from the car to the rave. Now I had known for a long time that my unwillingness to take harder drugs on the Reservation had made me the centre of discussion many times. But I never dreamt that they would spike my drink like this.

After about fifteen hours in hospital I felt fit enough to leave. Because we had arrived by ambulance, we had no choice but to walk back to the rave site. We had no money and no other means of getting there. Every step weighed a little more than the last. I felt really ill still and was emotionally a wreck. The journey felt like it would never end. When we eventually got back to the car, the site was still partying but by now it was late morning the next day. I stumbled the few final steps into the car and then set off for home.

Remarkably, as I was coming back from the hospital I passed Neil yet again. I stopped the car and he was still tripping. It turned out he had been trundling around the estate for thirty-six hours. Since the Friday night Neil had been tripping non-stop. He was still talking to himself in a confused manner, unable to stop walking or jittering on the spot. He reminded me of a child that had had far too many E numbers and was in some kind of hyperactive state.

The Reservation

So once again we left and watched him in the rear view mirror as he carried on trundling around the Reservation. I'm not sure how long he kept this up for but it was certainly an advert never to do Acid.

On the Sunday night at Torpedo Down, the ravers set fire to the power station next to the site the festival was being held on. So that ended up being the last proper free festival in the UK as the risks were now too high. Police dressed in riot gear came onto the site and started arresting everyone. It made the news on the TV and claimed that millions of pounds' worth of damage had been done but I heard it was just a temporary building. Never the less, no matter what the damage that night was, it was the beginning of the end for this free movement. Festivals would never be the same again after this.

That night really taught me what little shits my friends could be and how low they would go for a laugh at your expense. Just like when I was younger I felt singled out again for special treatment. This time I was not being physically bullied. This time they were trying to scar me in a deep, physiological way by spiking me. This night signified the beginning of the end of my raving days. It robbed me of one of the things I loved so much but I never again trusted the people I went out with. And to this day the physical and mental experiences from that night have weighed deeply on my mind. It really was a nail in the coffin that signified the end of my youth. After this happened to me everything suddenly became more serious. I started to worry a lot more and I began to distance myself from some of my degenerate friends.

By now we had all started to go our separate ways. But Neil and

Chaps would still come around my house without being wanted and Chaps could be a bit of an odd one at times. He had always been a bit special when I sat next to him at middle school. And he did have quite a sadistic and violent streak.

Those guys went everywhere together. People would ask have you seen Neil and Chaps? They were always a duo. Once, they were both in my house and Chaps said, "Give me a quid or I'll stab you." I laughed but then he pulled out a blade and said, "I need it, I ain't kidding." And then he snapped. His eyes turned grey and he had that 1,000-yard stare that combat troops often get after serving on the frontline. He looked so cold and evil, I couldn't tell if I was going to be stabbed to death for a pound or he was just joking about, as he was always high. I stood absolutely still and froze like a rabbit caught in the headlights. Chaps pushed me against the kitchen door and then said it again.

This time it was louder and scarier, "Give me a quid, I ain't fuckin with you." After a split second, that felt like an eternity, I replied, "I don't have any money." Chaps yelled, "Fucker," and then tried to stab me. Instinctively I shut my eyes as he thrust the knife towards me. My short life flashed before my eyes as I heard the blade rip into the door I was standing next to. Chaps screamed, "Last fucking chance." "Hold on, hold on, let me see what I can find." I was terrified. I had absolutely no money but ended up giving him a pair of silver earrings that belonged to my Mum.

All the time I was begging for him to put the knife away. "Sorted, those will do," said Chaps and looked really pleased with his prize. He then inspected his blade, folded the butterfly knife up and tucked it into the back pocket of his jeans. Incredibly we did a few hot knives and then Chaps and Neil left. I imagine Chaps traded the earrings for some kind of drugs.

Not long afterwards the Reservation was awash with news about a killing over the Christmas period. It made all the papers and was on the TV. Chaps had viciously stabbed someone to death in Southsea. There were hordes of police around his house and all over the Reservation looking for him. He had stabbed someone over twenty times on Boxing Day. I can only imagine the evil look on his face and that 1,000-yard stare I'd seen as he repeatedly plunged a knife into his victim. Then ripping it out, like some kind of savage, until they were lifeless.

Chaps was put on remand at Winchester Prison before going on trial but hanged himself. The funeral service was right next door to the petrol station and the house we had burnt down. A few people from the Reservation went to the funeral but I decided against it. It did however, make me realise for the first time that the Reservation was like a sponge. It was a twisted, empty void that soaked up everything around it. If you were not careful the Reservation lifestyle could get under your skin and turn you into a monster. Chaps was an all too familiar example of this. Drugs really do cause problems on places like the Reservation. They become a way of life or an escape route for the inhabitants.

Some people manage to use drugs only recreationally. Others start at the bottom and use them as a kind of ladder until they reach the top and die in one way or other. Death by drugs is not necessarily a physical thing. All too often you can still see the living but withered remains of people you once knew and loved. But now they are no more than a shell.

The Tripper

But I was lucky, I had Kath. After Kath and I started going out, in no time at all we were both completely at ease with each other and there were no restraints on our love. We would spend hours basking in awe of each other's company, lying in the park just holding hands, laughing and staring for hours at the lazy fluffy clouds, as they meandered across the sky. When we had the money we enjoyed going to the local pub, the cinema or the seaside. When I was working at the garage I was earning £80 a week while Kath was on a YTS scheme and earning just £30. After we had both paid rent and petrol we were always broke. Kath would often have to walk several miles to work and she had holes in her shoes and sometimes went without lunch.

Kath really made me feel alive. Every word, every touch, every moment we spent together. And I am pleased to say that she was the first woman I made love to. It was a very special experience for me and the earth moved for me. But my memories of this are mine and mine alone to enjoy. I am really pleased that I held on until things were right with the right girl and I was sure our relationship would last.

However, a lot of the lads on the Reservation used to have sex with anything, and when I say anything, I mean anything. Most of them lost their virginity and had their first sexual experience with a girl nicknamed The Trog. The Trog was fat and extremely grim looking with personal hygiene issues. She would often be found giving hand jobs in the woods or near the local pond. The fact she spent so much time on the scrubland near the pond was the reason she got her nickname. Often there were groups of people down there either taking turns or watching. Despite the peer pressure to sleep with 'something' I had decided early on that I wanted it to be with the right woman for the right reasons, and I stuck to it no matter what. I wanted to be in love with someone both physically and mentally as your first time was meant to be special.

I had to stop smoking puff in late 1993 after I started having panic attacks and it was making me paranoid. I don't regret it at all, but I'm pleased it came to an end just as the early 90s rave scene was dying off.

Thatcher had passed some law known on the streets as the 'three's a crowd law' to prevent illegal raves as the movement had gained so much momentum. And just like the generation on the Reservation, we were growing up. To this day I have never used any other drugs or even had another spliff. I even quit drinking for about fifteen years. Unfortunately, some of my friends were not so lucky and those years would set them on a path to self-destruction. For at least some these years would prove to be defining moments in their lives, dictated by the choices they made. But you could see that the drugs were taking over. Everyone was high or obsessing about being high, raving or taking drugs. It seemed to be the only thing that anyone ever wanted to do and everything was improved by drugs, work, nights out, even watching TV or eating. Everything revolved around being high. As I look back on those years now, most of them seem like a dream and I'm guessing that's because most of them were a dream.

Chapter Fourteen
The End of an Era

We tend to dismiss, out of hand, phenomena we don't understand; for fear of being ridiculed or labelled as some kind of freak. We simply try to forget those events as we don't like the thought of being unable to logically explain things. I just ask you to keep an open mind at the events that unfolded at Port Road.

I think most of us have witnessed something a bit surreal or unexplainable during our lives. One night, when I was a very small boy, around four or five, my Mum came upstairs with me to tuck me up in bed. As we opened the bedroom door, we both witnessed something that will stay with me until the day I die. As God is my witness we stood by the door and watched as about ten glowing orbs flew around the room. They were a variety of bright colours and each one was around the size of a large orange. They were really beautiful and the sight was hypnotic. Mum and I gasped in shock at what we were witnessing.

I was just an innocent child. My world was very small and I had no idea what these things were. At that age I just assumed they were some kind of fairies or magic. I watched in amazement as they stopped flying around the room and hovered; it was as if we were being observed. These things were beautiful; I mean really beautiful. The lights were so pure and the colours so vivid. I'm not really sure how to get the wonder of it all across on paper. But it was a spectacle that really affected me emotionally. It was like all my Christmases and birthdays put together.

After a few seconds, that felt like an eternity, the orbs flew around the room and then flew out the window in a straight line towards the sky. Mum and I ran to the window and watched until they were out of sight.

Now you could go mad thinking about what they were. I'm guessing it could range from some kind of ball lightning to spirits or even extra-terrestrials. Who knows? All I can say is that we both witnessed these events together. Mother and son, in the 70s, in my bedroom in a council house, in a normal road, in the dark; up close and personal. I will leave it at that. I don't really have any other opinions or wish to speculate about what it was. All I can say is that whatever it was, it was as real as the sun coming up in the morning. To get me off to sleep that night, my Mum told me they were my guardian angels. I guess it's a tough one to explain to a young child.

Years later I witnessed another strange phenomenon. The house in Port Road was nothing special. In 1994 it served as our very own doss house and general drop-in centre. This continued after Swain joined the navy and his Dad moved out after splitting up with his girlfriend. Des was renting it with a girl called Michelle and Cotton was renting a room. He had left home due to the continuing issues with his Dad. One time we were woken up at 3am by stones being thrown at my window. It was Cotton and Dale begging for refuge. I dragged my tired ass out of bed and let them in. They were visibly distraught and Cotton was shaking. I asked what on earth was going on and they said, "Real shit you will never believe." The police had been called. At this point a million thoughts were racing through my mind but none of them came close to what they were about to tell me.

One of the guys had found an old Ouija Board in the loft and they all thought it was a good idea to smoke a spliff and try it out. The first thing I assumed was that either one of them was playing a prank or the cannabis was playing with their minds. I mean that would be anyone's first thought, right? But Cotton was in tears as he told me about the events that followed. Apparently they had been talking to a spirit and everything on the Ouija Board had started moving on its own. All the lights in the room went out and the candles blew out at the same time. It freaked everyone out.

There were about six or seven people there and the house emptied in seconds flat, after 'the occurrence' happened. Everyone ran out into the street in a blind panic, screaming and crying. My friends were a lot of things but they weren't normally pussies. And Des was analytical and extremely reliable as far as witnesses go. The neighbours called the police, thinking there had been a murder or something. The police arrived to find everyone outside in a state of hysteria, screaming and crying. They did their best to explain what had happened but understandably the police had their doubts. I mean this house was known to have been raided by the police when Gal used to deal from it. However, one of the officers seemed to be quite sympathetic and went in the house to get a few of the guys' personal belongings.

What struck me as odd was that none of them would go back

in the house. Cotton and Dale crashed on the floor at mine and the next morning reluctantly asked if I could take them to the house to collect their stuff. When we arrived Des was standing outside trying to pluck up the courage to go in and get his stuff. He looked relieved when we all turned up as he was still visibly shaken and scared. He said he could never sleep under that roof again despite having paid a month's rent in advance. I made a joke about it being a pot spirit and went in first. It was fairly eerie. All the curtains were still drawn. Packets of cigarettes and half-finished drinks were still there along with cigarettes in the ashtray that had burnt out and turned into ash. A few bits of furniture were turned over and you could see evidence of the struggle to get out of the house.

Nevertheless, I continued to look around. The Ouija Board was still in position. There had been about four or five lit candles but what struck me as odd was the fact that the wax had gone vertically up the walls, like they had somehow been blown out from underneath. It was like a scene from the Mary Celeste. As the guys quickly packed up their stuff, there was a knock at the door. It was the sympathetic police officer from the night before asking if everything was okay.

He was invited in and his presence gave some much needed reassurance that everything would be okay, despite pot smoking paraphernalia being littered everywhere. The officer sat on the sofa next to me, facing the fireplace and the doorway to the kitchen, chatting to everyone as they packed up their stuff. Then all of a sudden, as God is my witness, the books on the shelf, next to the fireplace, started flying off the shelf, one by one. I witnessed it along with the officer and everyone else in the room. The officer shot up and ran out the door saying, "I have to get back to work." Then he jumped in his car and drove off. I sat there for a split second wondering if I had really seen what I thought I'd seen. Then the screaming started as everyone ran out of the house.

Poor Cotton had nowhere to live but wouldn't go back there. The place was abandoned and it was the end of an era. Several quick visits were made in groups, to collect belongings but no one would ever sleep in that house again. The house had something wrong with it but no one really knew what to do about it. I know it sounds like some kind of fairy tale. I myself thought it was a pot ghost until I witnessed the books flying off the shelves in broad daylight with a police officer sat next to me.

This was a house that had come to mean everything to us over the years. We all had a deep attachment to it and it had been our spiritual pot smoking home. But just like that, it was abandoned in an instant, never to be used by us ever again. I'm not sure what happened to it afterwards but I'm pleased I never lived there. I can't comment further as to what went on there, other than what I saw with my own eyes. I will let you draw your own conclusions. But even now, over twenty years later, those who were there that night refuse point blank to talk about it.

I have always had a massive interest in history. It is one of the few subjects I took an interest in at school and my Grandad died fighting for his country during World War II. It was also a hobby that cost absolutely nothing to do. It was 6th June 1994 and the 50th Anniversary of the D-Day landings by the allies on the French coast. Portsmouth had been a major embarkation port for D-Day and a few miles from us was the pretty village of Southwick and in it, Southwick House, which was the Allied Headquarters from where the whole invasion was planned. So it was playing host to a massive public celebration on Southsea sea front. There were all kinds of events, displays and things to do but I was particularly looking forward to the air display. As a child I had always romanticised about being a fighter pilot during the Battle of Britain. I used to have two polystyrene planes that were powered with elastic bands and would dogfight for hours in the lounge at home.

I'd been looking forward to this day for months. I'd managed to get the Saturday off and was excited about going to Portsmouth. I walked into the bathroom and was half way across the floor when I collapsed. As I came round I screamed for Kath. My chest felt like it was going to explode and breathing was extremely difficult. In the moments that followed I was sure someone was about to prematurely stamp my life card – time's up. I was begging Kath to call an ambulance but she was taking forever to decide whether to make the call. I guess she was worried or in shock. Seconds felt like an eternity, as I gasped for breath like a fish being pulled out the water.

I was taken to the Queen Alexandra Hospital where I was hooked up to an ECG and poked and prodded like a pin cushion. I was a 21-year-old man, in the prime of life, but inside I was a scared child. I lay in A&E, struggling to breathe and shaking like a leaf. I was in a state of shock and terrified. I had pins and needles in my hands and feet, felt hot and my skin was clammy. I was seen by a Doctor and told I had something called Rapid Atrial

The End of an Era

Fibrillation and was having a bad attack. My heart was beating at around two hundred and twenty beats per minute. From what I understand, the valves were opening and closing at the wrong times so that meant the blood wasn't pumping correctly. This was causing the numbness and shortness of breath.

It was a terrible day; one of those days you wish could be removed from your memory for the rest of your life. But instead the sheer panic at the time makes it more vivid and a permanent reminder of that day.

Later that afternoon, while they were trying to find me a bed, things started to ease off a little. I could feel my hands and feet again and the chest pain eased a little. Emotionally, this D-Day felt like I was trapped down a long dark tunnel. It was overwhelming and part of me already knew that moving forward, things might never be the same again. But I lay there and tried to think about all the good things in my life and all the things I still wanted to do. My goals, dreams, ambitions; my family, my friends but most of all Kath, who was squeezing my hand, and crying next to the bed.

As they explained I had to be admitted for more tests, I looked Kath straight in the eye, removed the oxygen mask and said, "No need to cry, please don't, everything will be just fine." And squeezed her hand. I was taken to a ward and monitored while they were waiting for a bed in the Coronary Care Unit. Kath's mum, Lucie, worked there as a Staff Nurse and popped in to see me. She held my hand and said, "Everything will be fine Mart, we are just trying to get you a bed upstairs." Lucie always had a reassuring way about her and I can tell you, she was a welcome sight for sore eyes.

After she left I was in bed, still shaking a little. It was now late afternoon and I remember thinking: this really is a day of days but not in a good way. My bed was right next to the window, a few floors up and facing towards the sea on the side of Portsdown Hill. As I looked out there wasn't a cloud in the bright blue sky. The windows were open and it was then I witnessed something spectacular. In the distance I could see lots of little dots coming towards us. It suddenly dawned on me it was the WWII aircraft finishing their display along the sea front and they were flying over the hospital on the route back to base. As they got closer and closer I could make out the different types of planes. There seemed to be endless amounts of Hurricanes, Spitfires, and Bombers. They were fairly low and thanks to a panoramic view of the city from my window, I could clearly see as the first two Hurricanes came towards us, tipped their wings and turned. For a brief moment, on this shitty day of days, my mind was released from all the pain, suffering and stress that had had been gripping my body since I woke up that morning.

Within minutes the ward was filled with the rich sound of those wonderful Merlin engines as more and more planes started to fly over. It was an orchestra of sound I never heard again. I was a child once more and closed my eyes for a split second and focused on that beautiful sound of victory. I could almost feel the vibrations of the planes' engines and imagined I was up there, in that wonderful blue sky, free as a bird with the whole world beneath me. In the moments that followed this spectacular event, I could feel my spirits lifting and noticed I had stopped shaking. Despite my current predicament I had mentally drawn a line in the sand and it was at that exact moment that I decided that if

The End of an Era

I got another chance at life, I would live it as good and as full as I could. As the last of these planes came towards me and tipped their wings, some of Sir Winston Churchill's famous words came to me, from the very depths of my mind. And I kept holding on to them and repeating them to myself over and over again. "Now this is not the end. It is not even the beginning of the end. But it is, perhaps, the end of the beginning."

In the weeks and months that followed, as I set about recovering, I gave up trying to sell cars on my own, and set about trying to better myself. I assumed that the most important purchase that people would ever make would be a house, so I set my mind on that as my next career move. The only problem was how on earth was I going to get a job as an estate agent? I picked up a copy of the Yellow Pages, opened the page for estate agents and one by one, I started cold calling all the local branches looking for work.

After a good few, "No sorry we can't help you," or "Do you have any experience?" I spoke to a Branch Manager at Cornerstone Abbey National in Drayton and used that powerful line, "I will work for free," that had won Colin over. And before I knew it we were laughing and joking on the phone. As he said, I was "so ballsy" that he arranged an interview with the Area Manager. And before I knew it, I was a Junior Negotiator for Cornerstone Abbey National in Drayton. Wow, by Reservation standards this was one hell of a deal. Within a year or so I had worked my way up to be a Senior Negotiator and was hoping that soon I would manage my own branch.

I wore a suit, had a company car and earned good money; well good money for those days! Kath and I were now earning enough to get our own place, away from the Reservation. We bought a little two-up two-down in Portsmouth. Although dilapidated we slowly made it into our own home. We were madly in love and had our whole life ahead of us. Finally, both mentally and physically we had escaped the Reservation.

Epilogue

This book has been so hard to write for so many reasons and on so many levels. Emotionally and physically it's hard to know where to start. It's been a dream and long-term goal for me to do for a number of years. Personally it's been a huge challenge for me to write this book as I was dyslexic at school and you probably won't be surprised that I got a 'G' in English. In fact, funnily enough, it has taken me several attempts to spell dyslexic well enough for the spell checker to even work out what I was trying to spell! This book is dedicated to my broken leg, without it and the constant crap on Sky TV, I doubt I would ever have been able to sit still long enough to finish it. But don't think that if you have enjoyed it that you need to become my number one fan, and break both my ankles to get a sequel, Misery style. Oh please!

So what happened to us all? Cotton ended up as a chef and straightened out his life and went on the straight and narrow, after losing his dear brother in a bike accident in Bournemouth. It was a cruel tragedy and it hit him really hard. His Dad recently died but he hadn't spoken to him for years. Nor did he go to his funeral. Hardly surprising after the cruel mental and physical abuse he suffered at his hand for all those long, dark years while growing up.

Cotton has no children, is single and still has his happy-go-lucky attitude. He claims to have had over five hundred jobs in the catering industry as he never really settles anywhere for long and seems to like the nomadic lifestyle. Or perhaps he is always running from something; who knows? Unfortunately, I have not managed to speak to him for several years since he decided to try working abroad. I hope he is well and I still think about him fondly.

Dale joined the navy but unfortunately ended up in Colchester Prison after being caught with drugs in Portsmouth one night. They gave him a blood test and said something like, "There are traces of blood in your ecstasy, Acid, speed and puff stream!" After he did his time he received a dishonourable discharge. Dale then started hanging around on the Reservation with the wrong kind of people. And he began taking heroin.

Over the last fifteen or so years I have done everything in my power to help him get clean but unfortunately he has really struggled with his addiction. I have lost count of the amount of times he has been through rehab. One time I saw him he looked like a dishevelled concentration camp survivor. The drugs had sucked the life out of him; he looked like a yellow, gaunt mess of a man. But recently he has been in touch and I believe he has met a girl and is now clean. I pray he stays that way. But I dread the phone ringing, and the voice at the other end asking me to attend his funeral. I really hope he sticks to his new path before it is too late. He is one of the most giving and kind people that I have ever known.

I bumped into Swain in Argos about ten years ago. He was living with somebody in Gosport and was running some kind of electrical component shop. We had a quick chat about old times

Epilogue

and exchanged numbers. Unfortunately, the number he gave me was wrong and he never contacted me. I hear he got married and is now living happily and he might even have children.

Fizz ended up going to university as a mature student after he left the navy. It must have been a real achievement for him to get a degree and I imagine he had to work really hard at it. I'm so proud of him. He is now working with the mentally ill and lives in Portsmouth. Occasionally we go surfing together in West Wittering and he is still great company after all these years. He has no children yet either; I'm guessing he is waiting for the right woman.

I bumped into Neil, the Incredible Bullshitting Man, one day and we have been close friends ever since. He barely looks any different to when I knew him all those years ago. He had a lot of menial jobs before deciding to retire, thanks to the tax payer, in his late 30s but then to everyone's surprise he recently got a job. He is still like a record stuck in the early 90s, when you talk to him but a great guy. He was living in terrible conditions on the Reservation but recently met someone and moved to a better area. He MCs and DJs in his spare time and I have to say he is really good at it.

Gal was living in a caravan near Wickham when I bumped into him a few years ago. We loosely keep in touch. He buys and sells stuff at car boot sales, when he's not having women problems; he seems to have a lot of women trouble. He recently started a drain clearance business and loves it. He is like a pig in shit! He is making good money now and has a couple of children that mean the absolute world to him. Things seem to have really turned around for him in the last few years.

Colin ended up in a very senior position with a large UK

company. He gets a great benefits package and seems really happy. He has a number of properties including an apartment abroad. We speak on the phone occasionally and always plan to meet up but never do. I am still really fond of him after all this time. In so many ways he will always be the father I never had.

Mandy met someone where she used to live and is happily married with a wonderful family. I don't know a lot more than that but I'm really pleased that things worked out well for her. I believe she used to race yachts as well.

Wes ended up marrying Laura who was also lodging at Port Road all those years ago. They have a wonderful family and it's no surprise that he has a highflying job in computers and ended up emigrating to Australia. We always knew deep down that this guy would come out on top. I always knew our adventures would be character building for him.

And as for me, I certainly never ended up as an English Teacher. But I married Kath in 1998 and we are still together after sharing so much together over all those years. And we are living happily in a beautiful house in the country. Unfortunately, we have never been blessed with children but we have four wonderful cats and two horses instead. We renewed our vows in 2013 so she made me the proudest man on earth twice. I had a few more jobs before starting my own internet company with one of my brothers. My adult life has been even more incredible than my childhood. I suppose you could call me an entrepreneur but it's been nothing but hard work, determination and pure drive to have the life today I dreamed about as a child. But hey, I am from the Reservation and that chapter of my life is another story altogether…

Also from Splendid Media...

A Dream To Die For
By Nicholas Faulkner

Mike Stapleford is a successful lawyer in his mid-forties. Married to a lovely woman, he lives an enviable existence and has little to complain about.

Sure, his marriage to Victoria isn't perfect, but then whose is? Everything changes when a vivid dream forces Mike to question his own mortality and what he wants from the rest of his life.

He has to face the question of what means most to him in this world and just what he wants to achieve before he dies...
£7.99 (paperback)

"a life affirming page-turner"

The Gift Room
By Nicholas Faulkner

Alexander had not spoken to his parents for more than 20 years, yet the news of their sudden deaths comes like a bolt from the blue. The loss forces him to address what's missing in his otherwise perfect life - an acknowledgement from them of his accomplishments... But how can that be provided from beyond the grave and what is the significance of The Gift Room?

Will Alexander finally be able to find the peace of mind that has eluded him for almost all of his adult life?
£7.99 (paperback)

Splendid
media group

Also available...

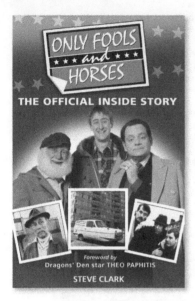

**Only Fools and Horses -
The Official Inside Story**
By Steve Clark
Foreword by Theo Paphitis

This book takes us behind the scenes to reveal the secrets of the hit show and is fully authorised by the family of its writer John Sullivan.

This engaging tribute contains interviews with the show's stars and members of the production team, together with rarely seen pictures.

Written by bestselling author Steve Clark, the only writer on set for the filming of *Only Fools and Horses*, *The Green Green Grass* and *Rock & Chips*, this book gives a fascinating and unique insight into this legendary series.
£9.99 (paperback)

The Official Only Fools and Horses Quiz Book
Compiled by Dan Sullivan and Jim Sullivan,
Foreword by John Sullivan

Now you can test your knowledge of the legendary sitcom in *The Official Only Fools and Horses Quiz Book*, which is packed with more than 1,000 brain-teasers about the show.

Plus there's an episode guide and an exclusive foreword by the show's creator and writer John Sullivan, who reveals some of the mystery behind the much-loved series and just how he came up with some of television's most memorable moments.
£7.99 (paperback)

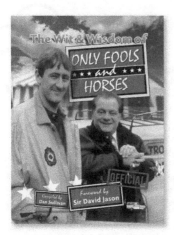

The Wit and Wisdom of Only Fools and Horses

Compiled by Dan Sullivan
Foreword by Sir David Jason

The 'crème de la menthe' of the hilarious one-liners from John Sullivan's *Only Fools and Horses* have been brought together for the first time in *The Wit & Wisdom of Only Fools and Horses*.

All of Del, Rodney, Grandad, Uncle Albert, Boycie, Trigger and the rest of the gang's funniest and most memorable lines are here, making this triffic book a pukka 42-carat gold-plated bargain.
£4.99 (paperback)

The British Television Location Guide

By Steve Clark and Shoba Vazirani

This beautifully illustrated book reveals the settings for dozens of top television shows. From *Downton Abbey* to *Doc Martin* and from *Midsomer Murders* to *Broadchurch*, the book gives details of how you can visit the places you have seen so many times on television. It includes details of the locations for more than 100 television series.
£9.99 (full colour paperback)

Catching Bullets: Memoirs of a Bond Fan
By Mark O'Connell, Prelude by Barbara Broccoli,
Foreword by Mark Gatiss and Afterword by Maud
Adams

When Jimmy O'Connell took a job as chauffeur
for 007 producers Eon Productions, it would
not just be Cubby Broccoli, Roger Moore and
Sean Connery he would drive to James Bond. His
grandson Mark swiftly hitches a metaphorical ride
on a humorous journey of filmic discovery where
Bond movies fire like bespoke bullets at a Reagan-
era Catholic childhood marked with divorce, a
closet gay adolescence sound-tracked by John
Barry and an adult life as a comedy writer still
inspired by that Broccoli movie magic.
£7.99 (paperback)

To order:
By phone: **0845 625 3045**
or online: **www.splendidbooks.co.uk**

By post: Send a cheque (payable to Splendid Books Limited) to:
Splendid Books Limited,
Diamond Suite, The Jubilee Hall, Little Shore Lane
Bishops Waltham, Hampshire SO32 1ED

Written a book? Find out how to get it published...

splendidmedia.co.uk

facebook.com/splendidmediagroup